Better Lesson Plans, Better Lessons

Practical Strategies for Planning from Standards

Ben Curran

Routledge
Taylor & Francis Group

NEW YORK AND LONDON

First published 2016
by Routledge
711 Third Avenue, New York, NY 10017

and by Routledge
2 Park Square, Milton Park, Abingdon, Oxon, OX14 4RN

Routledge is an imprint of the Taylor & Francis Group, an informa business

Library of Congress Cataloging-in-Publication Data
Curran, Ben.
    Better lesson plans, better lessons : practical strategies for planning from standards / by Ben Curran.
        pages cm
    Includes bibliographical references.
    1. Lesson planning.   2. Education—Standards.   I. Title.
    LB1027.4.C87 2016
    371.3028—dc23
    2015015831

ISBN: 978-1-138-83886-4 (hbk)
ISBN: 978-1-138-83887-1 (pbk)
ISBN: 978-1-315-73375-3 (ebk)

Typeset in Palatino
by Apex CoVantage, LLC

Better Lesson Plans, Better Lessons

In today's high-stakes world, using ready-made lessons and teacher's guides are no longer enough to guarantee achievement. The best way to help students succeed is through deliberate and careful lesson planning focused on the end result of increasing student achievement. Whether you are a new teacher or an experienced educator, this book will help you get started by providing a practical, step-by-step guide to designing lessons that will lead to student mastery of any objective. You'll learn the essential components of lessons that are Common Core-aligned and grounded in best practices. Topics include:

- Tailoring your lessons to meet your state standards while ensuring high student achievement.
- Writing a strong objective to stay focused on the goal of a lesson.
- Creating an end-of-lesson assessment to gauge the lesson's success.
- Constructing a lesson plan that combines direct instruction, guided practice, and independent practice.

Along the way, you'll find plenty of helpful examples from math and English language arts. You'll also find end-of-chapter FAQs and activities to try, to help you make these concepts a reality for your own classroom. Many of the tools from the book are also available as free downloads from our website (http://www.routledge.com/9781138838871/).

Ben Curran coaches school leaders for The Achievement Network, a national nonprofit dedicated to leveling the playing field in education. He previously worked as a teacher and instructional coach. Ben is also co-author of *Engaged, Connected, Empowered: Teaching and Learning in the 21st Century* (Routledge, 2014).

Engaged, Connected, Empowered: Teaching and Learning in
the 21st Century
Ben Curran and Neil Wetherbee

Classroom Instruction from A to Z, Second Edition
Barbara R. Blackburn

Motivating Struggling Learners: 10 Ways to Build Student Success
Barbara R. Blackburn

Rigor in Your Classroom: A Toolkit for Teachers
Barbara Blackburn

What Teachers Can Learn from Sports Coaches: A Playbook of
Instructional Strategies
Nathan Barber

What Schools Don't Teach: 20 Ways to Help Students
Excel in School and Life
Brad Johnson and Julie Sessions

Building a Community of Self-Motivated Learners: Strategies
to Help Students Thrive in School and Beyond
Larry Ferlazzo

Create, Compose, Connect! Reading, Writing, and Learning
with Digital Tools
Jeremy Hyler and Troy Hicks

Reinventing Writing: The 9 Tools That Are Changing Writing,
Teaching, and Learning Forever
Vicki Davis

Focus on Text: Tackling the Common Core Reading
Standards, Grades 4–8
Amy Benjamin

Writing Behind Every Door: Teaching Common Core
Writing in the Content Areas
Heather Wolpert-Gawron

Contents

Contents

eResources

The lesson plan template can be downloaded from our Web site so you can easily print it for your own use. You can access this download by visiting the book product page on our website: http://www.routledge.com/9781138838871. Click on the tab that says "eResources," and select the file. It will begin downloading to your computer.

About the Author

Ben Curran was born and raised in Pontiac, Michigan. He earned his teaching degree from Eastern Michigan University and began his teaching career in 2000. Since then, he has taught (at various times) fourth through eighth grades. He has also worked as an instructional coach, developing teachers around standards, planning, and practice.

Ben currently works in Detroit, Michigan, coaching school leaders for The Achievement Network, a national nonprofit dedicated to leveling the playing field in education. He is the coauthor of *Engaged, Connected, Empowered: Teaching and Learning in the 21st Century* from Routledge Eye on Education. His writing has also appeared in *Ed Week Teacher*, *Educational Horizons*, and on The Teaching Channel blog, *Tchers' Voice*.

Ben lives outside Detroit with his three children, Annabel, Bennett, and Leo.

Acknowledgments

There are so many people to thank. Without them, this book would never have been possible.

I have to start with my parents, Pam and David. Their support throughout the course of my life has never wavered. They never stop telling me how proud they are, either. I hope I do the same when it comes to telling them how much I appreciate and love them.

I would also like to thank my children, who not only light up my life but also give me another reason to want to support educators.

So many people have supported me professionally since the last book . . . I will try to note them all here:

> To Tamara Johnson, an incredible school leader. You believed in and trusted me as a teacher and a coach, which allowed me to grow in ways I never thought were possible.
>
> To Amrutha Nagarajan . . . you inspired me to do more and gave me the chance to make that happen.
>
> To Lawrence Hood, Kim Lijana, Lacey Slay and Elizabeth Horan Thompson, and all of my other colleagues at The Achievement Network. Not only did you put up with me during the writing process, but, more importantly, your collective brilliance and passion inspires me on a daily basis.
>
> To Amanda Rosman . . . you cofounded a school *and* find time to serve as my pro-bono legal counsel. Nothing short of amazing.
>
> To Neil Wetherbee . . . writing without you isn't the same. We are writing the next one together!

Finally, I'd like to thank anyone that has ever "suited up" and entered the arenas we call classrooms. You don't get enough credit for what you do. Your dedication to the most important of professions will continue to fuel my fire.

Introduction

If you don't know where you're going, you'll end up somewhere else.

—*Yogi Berra*

It seems unbelievable now, but when I began teaching in 1999, and for the next six or seven years after that, I was not required to turn in lesson plans. So I did what any young teacher would do—I didn't write them. That isn't to say that I didn't prepare to teach each day. Quite the contrary. I chose the page in the textbook, chose the homework, made the copies. I was prepared on a daily basis. But does that qualify as planning?

Looking back now, I definitely know that it does not. In my defense, it was a different era. The Common Core State Standards (CCSS) were not even close to being a blip on the radar—no one talked about how far behind the rest of the world American students were. No Child Left Behind (NCLB) wouldn't be passed for another few years—education was an issue left to states and municipalities to deal with.

Furthermore, "Schools of Choice," programs allowing parents to enroll their children in neighboring districts for free, were also nonexistent. The number of charter schools in my area could be counted on one hand. Standardized testing was merely a formality where I was working. In fact, we were encouraged "not to worry" about state tests. Conversations about performance-based teacher evaluations were still a decade away.

In that environment, my "planning" process was sufficient. I was a good enough teacher to know how to manage a class and communicate content to students. I knew how to ask good questions, and I knew when to ask them. My students performed well—even if I was flying by the seat of my pants.

But, oh, how things have changed. The CCSS and their national assessments are here—and here to stay. So are teacher evaluations that factor in student performance. In Detroit, where I work now, and in many cities across America, as many students, if not more, attend charter schools than traditional public schools (Lake, Jocim, and DeArmond 2015). Furthermore, not only do we have NCLB, but Race to the Top as well.

These factors, and others, have made teaching one of the most demanding jobs in the country. Increasing student achievement is job number one. If schools can't do that, they often face state takeover or worse (Hu 2011). So it becomes our charge as educators to find a way to make all of this happen—and as Yogi says, we certainly don't want to end up somewhere else.

Why then is this book needed? Because successful teachers and schools all over the country have shown that deliberate and careful lesson planning leads to effective lesson delivery. Because opening a textbook and reading word for word, assigning every problem, and giving a test at the end of the chapter just isn't enough. Because (perhaps most importantly) we owe it to our students. They deserve thoughtful, well-prepared lessons, day in, day out. What it comes down to is this: it is our plans that make or break our instruction.

Over time, however, the lesson-planning process has become complicated and cumbersome. Every pundit, professor, or professional development expert has a method and a template for creating the "perfect" lesson plan. Each district has its own format, too. And *that's* where this book comes in. In it, I will present a proven method for approaching lesson planning in a clear and (hopefully) easy-to-understand manner. Moreover, I base my approach not only on my experience as a classroom teacher and instructional coach, but on research-proven methods.

In the first part of the book, I'll examine two pieces of the puzzle that must be explored before a plan can even be created: the Common Core State Standards and summative assessments. These things define our desired outcomes for students. They represent where we want them to be when our teaching is done. Effective planning begins not at the start of the lesson, but at the end . . . of the class period, of the day, of the unit, and of the year.

The next part of the book will zoom in on two other important components that must be considered before the lesson plan can take shape: objectives and assessments. Both are vital pieces of the puzzle and both must be created before you can decide exactly what you and the students will do during the lesson.

The third part is where the rubber meets the road—when the planning of the actual teaching and learning takes place. I will guide you through the essential components of a solid lesson plan: direct instruction, and guided and independent practice. I will attempt to break these elements down into simple terms and to simultaneously describe what they look like in action, both from the teacher's and students' standpoints.

At this point, your lesson plan will be complete. Your daily work, though, isn't. The last part of the book looks at considerations that you must make once your lesson is complete. I'll explore questions such as: "What's next?" "What if they didn't get it?" and "How can I challenge high-achieving students?"

Along the way, you'll be provided with examples and activities for practicing these planning techniques, as well as appendices with a special note for school leaders and a planning template that can serve as a jumping-off point for you. My intent is to create a resource that you can follow along with while planning and also refer back to later on down the road.

The Common Core State Standards, coupled with the high-pressure environment of our profession, make thoughtful lesson planning a necessity. *Better Lesson Plans, Better Lessons* will serve as a practical, step-by-step guide for making this challenging (and often time consuming) process more effective and efficient.

Part I
Planning with the Standards in Mind

1

The CCSS and Lesson Planning

It takes as much energy to wish as it does to plan.

—Eleanor Roosevelt

The Common Core State Standards (CCSS) represent the most dramatic change to the field of education in a generation. They describe the end goal for students in each grade in Mathematics and English Language Arts (ELA). A book about lesson planning in the Common Core Era has to begin with an exploration of what the standards are all about. It's simple, really: in order to plan for students to meet the standards, we must first understand the standards themselves. While this may seem straightforward, it goes beyond knowing what students need to know by the end of the year. The content of the standards isn't difficult for teachers to understand. But there is more to it than that. The standards also call for instructional shifts, fundamental changes in the way content is delivered. These are critical for teachers to take into account when planning.

The shifts are described in great detail within the standards themselves (National Governors Association Center for Best Practices, Council of Chief State School Officers, 2010), but in this chapter I will provide a brief description of each, as well as an explanation of how each one impacts planning.

English Language Arts

Shift 1: Regular Practice With Complex Text and Academic Language

Exposure to complex text is critical in all grades, with each grade building upon the previous one. In every grade level, the CCSS call for students to

Figure 1.1 The three measures of text complexity

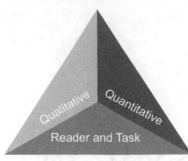

be exposed to complex, grade-level text. But, what exactly does that mean? Determining text complexity is, for lack of a better word, complex. The standards describe three measures for determining complexity: qualitative, quantitative, and reader and task. All three must be taken into account when selecting texts.

Qualitative measures require looking at the text itself: what challenges does it present in terms of language, knowledge demands, structure, and levels of meaning? Quantitative measures, such as Lexile levels, assess a text's readability and word count. Reader and task considerations include the reader's motivation and experiences, as well as the purpose of reading the text and the challenges of the questions asked about the text or the work assigned to go along with it. In essence, this third portion of complexity calls for teachers to use sound judgement in matching texts to readers and the tasks they are asked to perform.

When it comes to academic language, students should gain exposure to vocabulary that appears across content areas, as well as to subject-specific vocabulary. The CCSS call upon students to broaden their vocabularies through close examination of text, paying particular attention to words that will appear in other grade-level texts students might encounter.

Implications for Planning

Text selection matters. So in planning ELA lessons, it is critical that careful attention is paid to the text students will read. As Liben and Liben (2014) write, Shift 1 "will be a departure from what many teachers are accustomed to, which is the practice of always giving students 'just-right' texts, or leveled readers, as the core of their instructed reading."

When choosing texts in the planning stages, choosing grade-level complex text and giving all students access to it is imperative. This isn't to say that your reading lessons shouldn't be differentiated based upon students' reading abilities. They absolutely should be. However, instead of differentiation via giving different students different texts, the differentiation should take the form of offering differing levels of scaffolding and support.

When planning a reading lesson, two key questions should be asked about the text students will be working with:

1. What makes it challenging?
2. What do I want them to get out of it?

These questions provide a starting point and a means of choosing text in an efficient and straightforward manner. We don't always have time to do an in-depth qualitative evaluation of a text, or to look up its different quantitative scores. But with these two questions, we can begin to think about whether or not a text meets the grade-level demands of the standards, and make decisions accordingly.

A Note on "Letting Go"

I taught reading for a number of years. Anyone who does so develops a bank of "favorites," books that they love to teach with. However, the shift toward text complexity calls for all of us to reevaluate every text we use, even our favorites. This might mean that book you've been teaching characterization with for years isn't complex enough. For your students' sake, you might have to let it go.

Shift 2: Reading, Writing, and Speaking Grounded in Evidence from the Text

The second shift calls for students to regularly answer questions that require a close reading of the text. These text-dependent questions should go beyond surface-level questions, questions with answers that are directly stated, and questions that can be answered using prior knowledge, opinion, or experiences, to questions that require conclusions and inferences supported by the text. The same is true when writing or speaking about a text—student answers should be rooted in evidence from the text. See Table 1.1 for some example questions.

Implications for Planning

The big takeaway from Shift 2 should be the importance of text-dependent questions and supporting answers to these questions with evidence from the text. Text-dependent questions are questions that require students to

Table 1.1 Text dependent questions: Examples

NOT Text Dependent	Text Dependent
In "Casey at the Bat," Casey strikes out. Describe a time when you failed at something.	What makes Casey's experiences at bat humorous? Provide specific evidence from the text that supports your answer.
In "Letter from a Birmingham Jail," Dr. King discusses nonviolent protest. Discuss, in writing, a time when you wanted to fight against something that you felt was unfair.	What can you infer from Dr. King's letter about the letter that he received? Justify your response with citations from the text.
In "The Gettysburg Address" Lincoln says the nation is dedicated to the proposition that all men are created equal. Why is equality an important value to promote?	"The Gettysburg Address" mentions the year 1776. According to Lincoln's speech, why is this year significant to the events described in the speech?

Source: Student Achievement Partners (n.d., Achieve the Core)

return to the text after reading it to determine an answer. When planning, careful attention should be paid to the types of questions you'll be asking as well as the types of answers that will demonstrate mastery.

These two tips will help you ensure that your lessons meet the demands of Shift 2: read the text and write your questions in advance, and know Standard 1 for your grade level and the grades before and after. Let's dig into each of these in more detail to provide more context.

Tip 1: Read the Text and Write Your Questions (and Exemplar Answers) in Advance

Not only will this give you an opportunity to double check the text's complexity (see Shift 1), but it will help you ensure that you are asking students questions that will drive them toward mastery of the skills you are teaching. When writing questions it is important to consider Shift 2 and the push toward supporting answers with evidence from the text. It's also important to think of your questions as a group, rather than each in isolation. This will ensure that your questions build upon one another, scaffolding student understanding across the lesson in such a way that students are eventually demonstrating mastery independently.

Furthermore, taking the time to write exemplar answers to the questions you want to ask can greatly improve your lessons. These exemplar answers should represent what you want and expect to hear from students when they answer your text-dependent questions. With top-quality answers to your questions in mind before you ask them, you will then know during your lesson if students are demonstrating the understanding that you are working toward.

How can you make sure your questions meet the demands of Shift 2? Table 1.2 can serve as a guide.

Table 1.2 Checklist for text-dependent questions

Does the student have to read and return to the text to answer each question?

Is the student required to spend time lingering over a **specific portion** of the text?

Do the questions follow a coherent sequence, building toward deeper understanding?

Are the questions specific enough so they can be answered only by referencing the text?

For each question, does the student have to provide evidence from the text to support his or her answer?

Do questions focus on the most complex and challenging parts of the text? (These could be sections with difficult syntax, particularly dense information, and tricky transitions or places that offer a variety of possible inferences.)

Do students have the opportunity to practice speaking, listening to, and writing answers?

Adapted from Student Achievement Partners (n.d., Achieve the Core)

This provides a quick means of checking questions. Of course, questions should vary by grade, by text, and by standard.

A Note on Revising Questions

Many reading teachers work from a curriculum provided for them by their school or district. Lessons within this curriculum probably have questions written into them. However, just as we wouldn't buy a product simply because we saw an entertaining commercial for it, we should be careful not to ask questions about a text just because they're in the textbook. Use Table 1.2 to evaluate the provided questions, and revise as necessary. The extra work will pay off and translate into deeper understanding for your students.

Tip 2: Know Reading Standard 1

Reading Standard 1 describes the expectation for students when answering questions and providing supporting evidence. It, along with Reading Standard 10, forms a support for all of the other reading standards. In other words, Reading Standard 1 does not exist on its own, but rather it connects to and supports work in standards 2 through 9. If you think of the reading standards as a ladder, standards 2 through 9 form the rungs, with standards 1 and 10 representing the legs or rails. (See Figure 1.2.)

For this reason, a clear understanding of the expectations of Reading Standard 1 is important. You should understand Reading Standard 1 at your grade level so that you can not only write questions that align with grade-level

Figure 1.2 The Common Core Reading Standards

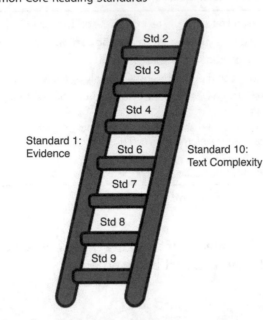

standards, but also so you can think about the answers students will give. Careful attention to Reading Standard 1, in your grade level and in the grades prior and following, will provide clarity when it comes to what types of answers students should provide to the text-dependent questions that you are asking. For example, if you're a seventh-grade teacher and you've been requiring students to provide a single piece of textual evidence in their answers, your students are actually meeting the sixth-grade standard. A close look at Reading Standard 1 in seventh grade reveals that seventh graders should "cite several pieces of textual evidence to support analysis." Knowing Reading Standard 1 is critical when it comes to making sure you are planning work for students that meets the requirements of their grade level.

Planning not only with text-dependent questions in mind but also the depth of student answers in mind will lead to stronger, more aligned lessons, where students are asked strong questions and are providing strong answers.

Reading Standard 1: Vertical Progression

College and Career Readiness (CCR) Anchor Standard 1: Read closely to determine what the text says explicitly and to make logical inferences from it; cite specific textual evidence when writing or speaking to support conclusions drawn from the text.

Kindergarten: With prompting and support, ask and answer questions about key details in a text.

Grade 1: Ask and answer questions about key details in a text.

Grade 2: Ask and answer such questions as who, what, where, when, why, and how to demonstrate understanding of key details in a text.

Grade 3: Ask and answer questions to demonstrate understanding of a text, referring explicitly to the text as the basis for the answers.

Grade 4: Refer to details and examples in a text when explaining what the text says explicitly and when drawing inferences from the text.

Grade 5: Quote accurately from a text when explaining what the text says explicitly and when drawing inferences from the text.

Grade 6: Cite textual evidence to support analysis of what the text says explicitly as well as inferences drawn from the text.

Grade 7: Cite several pieces of textual evidence to support analysis of what the text says explicitly as well as inferences drawn from the text.

Grade 8: Cite the textual evidence that most strongly supports an analysis of what the text says explicitly as well as inferences drawn from the text.

Grades 9–10: Cite strong and thorough textual evidence to support analysis of what the text says explicitly as well as inferences drawn from the text.

Grades 11–12: Cite strong and thorough textual evidence to support analysis of what the text says explicitly as well as inferences drawn from the text, including determining where the text leaves matters uncertain.

Shift 3: Building Knowledge Through Content-Rich Nonfiction

This shift is probably the most widely known of the three. The CCSS call for a balance between informational text and literature. The emphasis on informational text does not mean that literature should not play a role in literacy instruction. It does mean that, as students get older, a balance between the two is imperative. It also means that, in all grades, informational text should play a role in all subject areas.

By high school, the standards call for the ratio of informational text to literature to reach 70–30, with a 50–50 balance achieved in elementary grades.

Implications for Planning

The following questions are helpful to ask when planning for English Language Arts:

1. What is my balance of informational text and literature?
2. Am I paying attention to the specific language of the standards themselves—especially Standard 10?
3. Am I using informational text in subject areas such as social studies, science, and the arts?
4. Does the informational text that I'm planning to use aid in developing students' knowledge of the world around them?

This requires teachers to take a broad view, to look at the arc of the entire school year and the types of texts they are using throughout. Pulling back in this way, stepping up onto the balcony to look down at the year's plans, is important so that the proper balance of informational text and literature is maintained.

It can also be helpful to understand exactly what is meant by the phrase *informational text*. This can include an array of genres, from historical and scientific texts; to literary nonfiction such as memoirs, biographies, and autobiographies; to technical documents such as directions or manuals. It can even include nontraditional "texts" such as video or multimedia presentations. The key, according to Maloch and Bomer in "Informational Texts and the Common Core: What Are We Talking about, Anyway?" is that teachers should "open up the world of *books that teach* to students and . . . involve them in the categorizing, to ask them to discriminate among the many types of books that purport to tell the truth about the world" (2013).

Mathematics

Shift 1: Focus Strongly Where the Standards Focus

This shift calls for the elimination of a "mile wide, inch deep" approach to mathematics by narrowing the number of topics and concepts that students are expected to master in each grade. So that students develop a foundational understanding of mathematics, work should focus on the major areas of each grade, which are specifically named in the CCSS.

To achieve this shift, authors of the math standards reorganized topics, moving some out of grades in which they were traditionally taught and into others. One classic example is probability. Traditionally an area of study in fifth grade, probability has been moved to the middle school standards. In some cases, too, topics and specific strategies were removed entirely. Take for example, prime factorization, which is not named in any grades' standards. See Table 1.3 for a summary of the topics covered in grades K–8.

Table 1.3 High-level summary of major work in grades K–8

K–2	Addition and subtraction—concepts, skills, and problem solving; and place value
3–5	Multiplication and division of whole numbers and fractions—concepts, skills, and problem solving
6	Ratios and proportional relationships; early expressions and equations
7	Ratios and proportional relationships; arithmetic of rational numbers
8	Linear algebra and linear functions

Source: Student Achievement Partners (n.d., Achieve the Core)

Implications for Planning

An understanding of this shift is crucial in planning effective mathematics instruction. Whereas in the three ELA instructional shifts the order of implementation isn't critical, in math focus has to come first. If teachers are not focusing where the standards focus, it doesn't matter if they're designing effective, coherent, and rigorous lessons. Due to this, there are two key questions that must be taken into account when planning:

1. What's In and What's Out?

In terms of this first question, it's important to note what topics and concepts are part of the grade-level standards. There are some topics that tend to "hang around" in district curricula or in math textbooks that no longer apply to that grade level. When planning a lesson, it's a critical first step to ensure that what you are teaching is what you should be teaching.

2. What Category Is It In?

This second question digs a little deeper and requires some background knowledge of how the math content standards are arranged. They are grouped into domains and clusters, as seen in Figure 1.3.

The clusters themselves are categorized in a very important way. They are grouped into major, supporting, and additional clusters. *Major clusters* represent the "major work of the grade," the content to which a majority (at least 70 percent) of the instructional time should be devoted. *Supporting clusters* are important, but should be taught in a way that connects them to the major work of the grade. *Additional clusters* lie outside of the major work of the grade, but are key because they build a foundation for important standards in future grades.

Figure 1.3 The Common Core Mathematics Standards

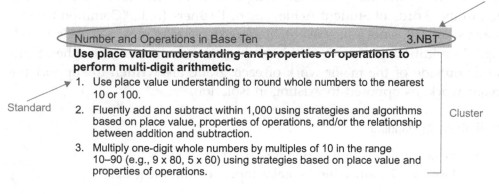

Domain

Number and Operations in Base Ten   3.NBT

Use place value understanding and properties of operations to perform multi-digit arithmetic.

Standard

1. Use place value understanding to round whole numbers to the nearest 10 or 100.

2. Fluently add and subtract within 1,000 using strategies and algorithms based on place value, properties of operations, and/or the relationship between addition and subtraction.

3. Multiply one-digit whole numbers by multiples of 10 in the range 10–90 (e.g., 9 x 80, 5 x 60) using strategies based on place value and properties of operations.

Cluster

This knowledge can impact planning because you want to make sure you are prioritizing your time effectively by doing these things:

1. Devoting a majority of your time to the major clusters
2. Connecting supporting clusters to the major work of the grade
3. Teaching additional clusters to support future work

A Note on the Language of the Standards

While it doesn't technically qualify as part of the shift of focus, paying attention to the language of the standards is critical and something I take into consideration after asking myself the two focus questions (In or out? Which cluster?). Zooming in on the specifics of each standard can illuminate exactly where you need to build to with your plans. Picking out key words and important details when planning will help you align your lessons and expectations to the CCSS.

For example, 3.NBT.3:

"Multiply one-digit whole numbers by multiples of 10 in the range 10–90 (e.g., 9×80, 5×60) using *strategies based on place value and properties of operations*." (Italics added)

Note that values are limited to 10–90 and also that strategies based on place value and properties of operations need to be used. This sheds light not only on what to cover, but also on the idea that we really need to help students understand the multiplication, rather than teaching them the trick of "adding on a zero at the end."

Shift 2: Coherence: Think Across Grades and Link to Major Topics Within Grades

From grade to grade, the CCSS in mathematics connect. This allows students to build upon material previously taught in an efficient and effective manner. In the words of Student Achievement Partners (n.d., "Common Core"), "each standard is not a new event, but an extension of previous understanding." In addition, standards within each grade connect to each other. Standards outside of the major work of each grade are written to support the major work, as opposed to existing in isolation.

Implications for Planning

1. How am I building upon work from prior years?
2. How am I connecting to major topics within the grade?

Thinking about these two questions is not the easiest thing for teachers to do. However, seizing every opportunity possible to illuminate and call out these connections for students can truly help to deepen their understanding of mathematics. Of course, this requires teachers to move from thinking only about their own grade-level standards to thinking about the standards that precede and follow their grade. This type of vertical thinking, combined with paying attention to how the standards within a grade are connected to one another, can help students process and internalize the work that you are calling upon them to do.

Shift 3: Rigor—in Major Topics, Pursue Conceptual Understanding, Procedural Skill and Fluency, and Application with Equal Intensity

Shifting toward rigorous work in mathematics does not mean assigning more work, moving concepts up so they are taught earlier, or assigning harder problems (Alberti 2012/2013). Rather, it involves a balance of three areas: deep conceptual understanding of major topics; fluent, accurate, and speedy performance with basic calculations; and application of math concepts in problem-solving scenarios. (See Figure 1.4.) The key word here is *balance*. That isn't to say that every single lesson should be balanced in terms of these three categories. However, looking at the entire course of study for a grade level, a balance should exist.

A quest for balance amongst these three categories cannot be accomplished without an understanding of what each of these three categories really means. Entire books could be written explaining these ideas. For the sake of brevity (and your sanity), though, I will sketch each one out briefly.

Figure 1.4 The three components of rigor

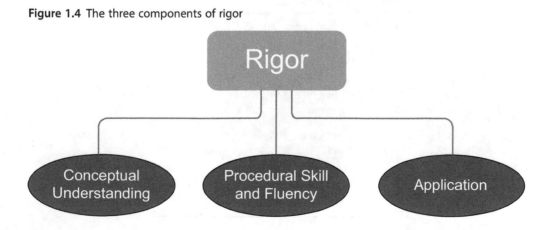

Conceptual Understanding

This refers to students' deep understanding of how and why mathematics works the way it does.

When building students' conceptual understanding, teachers should emphasize what the math means rather than relying on shortcuts or tricks. Take, for example, division of fractions. Teaching students to "multiply and flip" might allow them to quickly solve these types of problems, but it does not help them understand exactly what they're doing and what it really means to divide fractions. Other means, such as visual models, will work to deepen students' understanding of what is happening when you divide a fraction by a fraction.

Procedural Skill and Fluency

The CCSS do not ignore the importance of speedy calculation. Written into them are requirements for fluency in grades K–6, as Table 1.4 illustrates.

Application

This aspect of rigor calls for the inclusion of what are often referred to as "real-world" problems. Students should not only understand mathematical processes, but also recognize how they can be applied in the world around them.

Implications for Planning

1. Am I relying on tricks and procedures instead of focusing on conceptual understanding?
2. Am I providing opportunities to build fluency?
3. Am I helping students apply this work to real-world contexts?

Table 1.4 Calculation fluency in grades K–6

Grade	Required Fluency
K	Add/subtract within 5
1	Add/subtract within 10
2	Single-digit sums and differences (sums by memory by end of grade) Add/subtract within 100
3	Single-digit products and quotients (products by memory by end of grade) Add/subtract within 1,000
4	Add/subtract within 1,000,000
5	Multi-digit multiplication
6	Multi-digit division Multi-digit decimal operations

Again, these implications apply in a year-long context. They do not have to be a part of every single lesson. Nor, in fact, will they apply to every single standard. A close examination of the language of your grade-level standards will reveal which standards are intended to build conceptual understanding, which are meant to build fluency, and which should be applied to the context of the world around us. The key for teachers when planning is that they read the standards carefully to know when each aspect of rigor is in play.

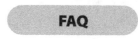

FAQ

This is a lot! How can I do it all?

I agree, the shifts can seem daunting. The key, though, is to remain mindful of them in your planning and your teaching. Keep them in the front of your mind as you plan and teach, and your work will become more aligned to the expectations of the CCSS. Knowing your grade level standards is certainly important. But you shouldn't think that you need to memorize them or be able to recite them backwards and forwards. What is critical, though, is understanding these shifts, for the shifts embody what the CCSS are really about. The more you take them into account in your work as a teacher, the more prepared your students will be for subsequent grades.

How do I read complex text with struggling readers?

There is no easy answer to this question. But it's a question that many teachers ask—and rightfully so. Not all sixth graders, for example, are ready or able to interact with and understand sixth-grade level text. While this is not a simple thing to do, it is important that you try to both meet students where they're at—by working with them using texts that they can access—and expose them to complex grade-level texts. For students who are reading below grade level, this will obviously require a great deal of scaffolding and support. You may need to build up to grade-level text in a deliberate and well-thought-out fashion. It is key, however, to provide students with as many opportunities as possible to work with grade-level text. They are going to need more support, of course, than your on-grade-level readers—and that's OK. Helping them to access these types of text is an important step in preparing them for the following grade.

What does any of this have to do with writing a lesson plan?

I would argue that these have everything to do with writing lesson plans. To write a lesson plan that is truly aligned to the Common Core State

Standards, you must know the instructional shifts that the CCSS call for. Evidence of this should be reflected in your plans, whether it be fluency practice or problems that apply to the "real world" in math or the types of questions you are asking about a text in ELA. Without an understanding of these shifts, your lesson plans may be mired in the way things have "always been done." Once you process and internalize the shifts, your lessons will organically become more aligned to the expectations of the Common Core.

Activity: Bring the Shifts to Life

Attempting to accomplish every shift all at once could quite possibly be a fool's errand. Instead, start small. Choose one and think about what your current practice looks like, then think about some small revisions that you could make in your practice that would aid you in making this shift. The note catcher in Table 1.5 may help you as you do this.

Table 1.5 Note catcher for instructional shifts

Instructional shift	What does your current practice look like in this area?	How could you revise what you're currently doing to better align with this shift?

The Role of Assessments

> You can't connect the dots looking forward; you can only connect them
> looking backwards.
>
> —*Steve Jobs*

In the Introduction, I confessed to rarely writing lesson plans early in my
career. Allow me to offer up another embarrassing truth from my teaching
past: I rarely gave any consideration to end-of-unit assessments until it was
time to administer them. I didn't look them over before starting the unit. I
didn't examine them midway through the unit to make sure I was on the
right track. I didn't even take a peek at the end to make sure I had covered
all the necessary content. How silly of me! What a wealth of vital information that was escaping me.

In this chapter, you'll explore how assessments can impact the lesson-
planning process. Subsequent chapters will walk you through the process
itself. Before that, though, it's important to think in a backwards fashion by
looking at items from summative assessments so that you can start thinking
about what it will take for students to master them.

The Role of Assessments

You see, it's the assessments that are the key to effective planning.
Whether you're using those provided by a textbook or creating your
own, whether you're looking at summative unit tests or weekly quizzes, the

assessments essentially tell you everything to know about how to plan effectively. So we begin each planning cycle at the end, looking backwards from the assessment, to figure out what we need to teach, and how to teach it.

This idea isn't a new one. In their groundbreaking book *Understanding by Design*, Grant Wiggins and Jay McTighe argue that "the specifics of instructional planning—choices about teaching methods, sequence of lessons, and resource materials—can be successfully completed only after we identify desired results and assessments and consider what they imply. Teaching is a means to an end. Having a clear goal helps to focus our planning and guide purposeful action toward the intended results" (2005, 19).

While this is an excellent approach in theory, planning backwards from assessments can prove incredibly challenging. Without a structured approach, looking at a test can leave a teacher bewildered as to where to start. It is a process that requires the teacher to become an instructional designer—and this is no easy task.

Compounding the challenge is one key requirement: A quality lesson plan cannot be created without a quality assessment. In this case, what we speak of is an end-of-unit assessment (also called a *summative* assessment). This assessment must be in hand at the outset.

There is, of course, much more to it than even that. Adoption and implementation of the Common Core State Standards, and their accompanying tests created by the Partnership for Assessment of Readiness for Colleges and Careers (PARCC) and the Smarter Balanced Assessment Consortium (SBAC), have raised the bar for assessments. Gone are the days when students can prove what they know about multiplication by completing several basic problems, or by answering problems on a reading test that require the location of explicit information in a text. The CCSS have ushered in richer, more challenging problems, problems that push students to reason, analyze, and support and explain their thinking. Even if you are in a state that has not adopted the Common Core, or you teach a non-CCSS subject, assessments have shifted to assess students' critical thinking skills more effectively and in a more rigorous fashion. With that in mind, an effective plan begins with an effective (and rigorous, standards-aligned) assessment.

This chapter makes the assumption that you have such an assessment in hand. (The rationale behind this assumption is that a guide on creating this kind of assessment would fill several hundred pages on its own.) From there, you can build effective plans—plans that will lead your students to demonstrate mastery of the assigned skills and of the required standards.

Parts 2 through 4 of this book will walk you through the specific components of a lesson plan. But first, we must look at the role of assessments.

Considering Assessments When Planning

Four key questions form the backbone of an assessment analysis:

- ◆ What skills are being assessed?
- ◆ How are these skills being assessed?
- ◆ What potential misunderstandings exist?
- ◆ What sequence and pacing should be used to teach these skills?

All of these questions should be answered before the writing of plans can begin. Let's examine each of these questions in more detail.

What Skills Are Being Assessed?

Before writing a single lesson plan, it is critical to comb through the assessment to determine the skills required for mastery. Sometimes, this is very straightforward. Other times, though, assessment items can be "unpacked" to reveal that several skills must be taught for mastery of a single item.

The skills should be recorded as learning targets, which are statements written in student-friendly language, beginning with "I can . . .", that identify what students will be able to do to answer this question. Learning targets serve as a sort of GPS for both teachers and students, guiding them toward mastery (Moss, Brookhart, and Long 2011).

Moss and Brookhart (2012) also argue: "the most effective teaching and the most meaningful student learning happen when teachers design the right learning target for today's lesson and use it along with their students to aim for and assess understanding" (p. 2).

(Writing effective learning targets will be covered in more depth in Chapter 3.)

How Are These Skills Being Assessed?

This critical question is often overlooked. You must make note of how each skill is being assessed. For example, if it's a math question, is it assessed through a simple problem (e.g. 345 × 25) or through a word problem? An

ELA example might involve the skill of identifying details that support a main idea. This could be assessed in a straightforward manner: "Which of the following details supports the main idea?" But the question could also be asked in a slightly more rigorous fashion: "Which of the following details does *not* support the main idea?" This subtle difference must be taken into account.

What Potential Misunderstandings Exist?

This is yet another overlooked consideration. In examining assessment items prior to planning, it is crucial to think about what misunderstandings students might have. If a question asks students to identify a metaphor in a passage and another asks students to identify a simile, a reasonable misunderstanding would be to confuse the two. If a math assessment asks students to evaluate 2 raised to the 4th power, one misunderstanding would be to multiply 2 times 4 rather than 2 times 2 times 2 times 2. Identifying these misunderstandings prior to planning will help you keep these things in mind as you write your plans, essentially heading off potential errors before students can make them.

What Sequence and Pacing Should Be Used to Teach These Skills?

At this point you are ready to map your unit. You'll have to decide how many lessons to devote to each skill, and the order in which to teach them. In some cases, there's no right or wrong answer to these questions—especially in terms of pacing. Once instruction begins, you may find that your pacing expectations need to be revised. For example, if you plan to use three lessons to teach a skill and students demonstrate mastery after the first day, you'll obviously adjust your pacing and move forward. More likely is a scenario where students struggle with a skill, and you must reteach it the following day. (For more on these situations, see Chapter 8.)

Sequence decisions require a careful eye, though. Order matters in almost all cases. For example, in the example question on supporting details described earlier, you'll need to be sure to teach students to identify the main idea of a passage first, and then teach them about supporting details.

The question of how to pace your units is often challenging to answer. Many of your decisions will be based upon prior experience.

Table 2.1 shows what one teacher's note-taking document might look like for assessment analysis.

Table 2.1 Example note catcher for assessment analysis

#	Skill being assessed (i.e. learning target to teach)	How it's assessed (e.g. multiple choice, open response)	Potential misunderstandings	Notes on sequence and pacing

Exploring a Math Assessment Item

Let's zoom in on a single assessment item to explore this process in action. Figure 2.1 shows a sample item released by the SBAC. It is a third-grade math question.

Figure 2.1 Third-grade math question from SBAC

Look at point *P* on the number line.

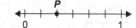

Look at number lines A – E. Is the point on each number line equal to the number shown by *P*? Choose Yes or No.

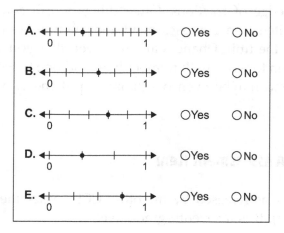

To begin, *what do students have to be able to do to answer this question successfully?* There seem to be two different skills that yield two different learning targets:

◆ I can label fractional segments on a number line between 0 and 1.
◆ I can identify equivalent fractions from a number line or illustration.

It is next important to consider *how these skills are being assessed*. This is not a straightforward, multiple-choice question. Nor is it a question requiring students to explicitly name or identify equivalent fractions. This is important to consider as we plan our lessons for this question. Students *do* need to learn how to label a number line with fractional amounts. They *do* need to understand equivalent fractions. But they also need to be able to match points on number lines to one another. When planning lessons, this needs to be taken into account. This is not to say that questions exactly like this one need to appear in the plans. It does mean, however, that students' understanding of this concept must be complete enough for them to transfer what they know to this challenging scenario.

Our third step is to *consider possible misunderstandings*. In this case, one potential misunderstanding is that all of the choices should be "no" because none of the points in A–E are located on the second tick mark like Point P is. Knowing your students, you will be able to think of others, too. It's important that you consider their past work when determining what they might struggle with.

Finally, we must decide *how much time to dedicate to this assessment item*. This is based on a number of factors, including students' previous experience with and knowledge of fractions. Other things worth considering are the total number of items on the assessment and the number of teaching days available during the unit. Chances are, however, that you would expect to plan for one lesson to work with number lines and one to work with equivalent fractions—and maybe even one more to put the two of these things together.

Exploring an ELA Assessment Item

The item below was released by the other CCSS assessment organization, the PARCC (2015). It is a seventh-grade item.

You have read two texts and watched a video describing Amelia Earhart. All three include information that supports the claim that Earhart was a daring, courageous person. The three texts are:

◆ "The Biography of Amelia Earhart"
◆ "Earhart's Final Resting Place Believed Found"
◆ "Amelia Earhart's Life and Disappearance" (video)

Consider the argument each author uses to demonstrate Earhart's bravery.

Write an essay that analyzes the strength of the arguments related to Earhart's bravery in at least two of the texts. Remember to use textual evidence to support your ideas.

This complex performance task requires a lot from students. *What do they have to be able to do?* The learning targets at play here might be written as such:

◆ I can identify an author's argument.
◆ I can analyze the strength of an argument using textual evidence.
◆ I can write an essay that articulates the strength of an argument in multiple texts.

This third learning target can be broken down further because so many different skills go into writing an essay. These more specific targets could be determined by a team of teachers and might include, among others:

◆ I can write a clear thesis statement.
◆ I can write a paragraph with a topic sentence and supporting details.
◆ I can use transition phrases to link my ideas together.
◆ I can write an essay with an introduction, body paragraphs, and conclusion.

This item is obviously very different from the math item. *How is it being assessed?* The critical consideration in this case is that students must synthesize information from multiple sources, including a video. Students must learn how to do this and this should be reflected in the plans.

In the case of possible misunderstandings, one that jumps out is that students might choose to *describe* the arguments rather than analyze them. This single possibility seems simple, but it is critically important and must be taken into consideration when planning lessons. Teaching students how to analyze an argument must be front and center during this unit.

When it comes to the fourth question, "how much time should be spent teaching these skills?" the short answer is "all that you can." Seriously, though, you will have to pace and sequence according to how many skills you need to teach students.

FAQ

This approach works if I have a high-quality, rigorous, CCSS-aligned assessment. But what if I don't?

Hopefully you have *something* to work from. If so, you can modify this existing assessment to create something that assesses deeper understanding. If you don't have an assessment, though, it's critical that you make one. Planning without an assessment to serve as a guide will lead to ineffective and scattered plans. In short, you have to know where you want them to end up or you won't be able to plan the best route to get there.

I'm using a textbook for the subject(s) I teach. Why do I need to analyze the assessments before writing lesson plans? Aren't the textbook-provided assessments enough?

You'd be surprised how frequently textbook-created assessments don't match the work or the level of rigor of the lessons prescribed by the textbook. Assuming that the textbook's lessons and its assessments align is a leap of faith—and it's the type of leap we want to avoid when student achievement is on the line. You still need to analyze them to make sure your teaching is going to provide adequate support for students.

Unfortunately, no . . . sometimes these assessments aren't enough. Or sometimes they aren't aligned with the goals of your school or district. Furthermore, when you factor in what the Common Core calls for in terms of student work or what the SBAC or PARCC assessments call upon students to know, they might not line up either (even if the textbook claims to be "CCSS-aligned").

Writing lesson plans is a time-consuming process as it stands. Why invest even more time in examining the assessments?

Consider this . . . do your current assessments reflect what your students actually understand and what they know how to do? Do your current assessments make an accurate statement about your students' mastery of the Common Core State Standards? If your answer is an honest "yes," then consider yourself lucky. If, however, you're like most of us and you can't answer "yes" to those questions, then this is sure to be time well spent. Furthermore, the time invested in analyzing assessments (and following the steps laid out in the following chapters) will actually save you time during the writing of your lesson plans.

Doesn't this approach ask teachers to simply teach to the test?

It most certainly does. But the key is that this method calls upon teachers to teach to an "authentic test," an assessment that will "test those capabilities and habits we think are essential, and test them in context" (Wiggins 1989). Teaching to a standardized test is not authentic practice. Wiggins continues:

> "Rather than seeing tests as after-the-fact devices for checking up on what students have learned, we should see them as instructional: the central vehicle for clarifying and setting intellectual standards. The recital, debate, play or game (and the criteria by which they are judged)—the "performance"—is not a checkup, it is the heart of the matter; all coaches *happily* teach to it. We should design academic tests to be similarly standard setting" (1989, 42).

In essence, if the test is an accurate and authentic measure, you should absolutely teach to it, and use it as your guide during the planning process.

Activity: Auditing Your Plans Using an Assessment Item

1. Select an assessment item from an upcoming unit assessment that you plan to use.
2. Break the item down by using the questions in Table 2.1:
   a. What skills are being assessed?
   b. How is it assessed?
   c. What potential misunderstandings might students have?
   d. What sequence or pacing considerations should be made?
3. Audit the lesson plans you have written that align to this item. Do they take everything you uncovered in Step 2 into account? If not, make the appropriate revisions.

Activity Extension

You can also repeat this activity by finding released assessment items from the PARCC, the SBAC, or your state's annual summative assessment.

Part II
Before the Lesson

3

Writing Objectives

Failure to hit the bull's-eye is never the fault of the target.
—*Gilbert Arland*

The best lessons start with a single sentence. A learning objective, sometimes called a *learning target* or *aim,* is the sentence that clearly and succinctly describes what students will be able to do at the end of the lesson. In essence, it answers the question "What will students be able to do after this lesson that they couldn't before it?"

Writing a strong objective may seem like a fairly straightforward task, but it takes a great deal of thought and care. A lesson with an objective that is not focused or not specific or not measurable will lead to teaching that leads students down winding paths and often to confusion, rather than understanding. Before you can plan your instruction, you have to know exactly what it is you are teaching.

It is important at this point to clarify the difference between "goals" and "objectives." They are not the same thing, as Mishra writes in *Lesson Planning:* "Goals are broad and difficult to directly measure . . . they help us focus on the big and important picture," but they do not describe what students will do or accomplish during a lesson (2009, 37). The same is true with standards and assessments. An understanding of each is critical, as explained in chapters 1 and 2. However, they alone do not represent what a teacher plans to accomplish in a single lesson. That is the function of an objective.

In this chapter, I will describe the key characteristics of strong objectives, as well as guidance around where objectives come from. I will start with purpose and then describe a process for writing strong objectives. These steps, and the steps described in Chapter 4 on end-of-lesson assessments, are critical pieces that are worth your—and your students'—time.

Qualities of Strong Objectives

A strong learning objective should be four things: measurable, bite-sized, clear, and aligned. Let's look at each one individually.

Measurable

For an objective to be measurable, it must describe something that you can assess at the end of the lesson. There has to be a means of measuring student success, otherwise you will have no idea if students can do what you taught them. A measurable objective allows you to accurately describe how well the lesson worked, which students learned what you taught them, and which ones didn't.

By making sure your objectives are measurable, you will avoid having to make assumptions about what your students know and don't know. A common pitfall, described by Doug Lemov in his book *Teach Like a Champion*, is for learning objectives to be written about understanding, appreciating, or other things that can't be measured: "If your goal is to have students know something or understand something or think something, how you will know they have reached it?" (2010, 61) Rather than teach these objectives, teachers should craft aims by which mastery can be demonstrated with evidence.

Bite-Sized

A bite-sized objective is one that can be achieved during the course of a short period of time, such as a single lesson. Larger objectives, that require long amounts of time to teach, restrict a teacher from learning about their students' understanding. Directly connecting to the "measurable" trait, objectives that aren't bite-sized can be difficult to measure. When that is the case, instruction becomes less flexible and it becomes challenging to make adjustments to what students need academically.

A common pitfall in this regard is for teachers to use the full language of a particular standard as a learning objective. For example, "Students will be able to use multiplication and division within 100 to solve word problems in situations involving equal groups, arrays, and measurement quantities" (Common Core State Standards in Mathematics, or CCSS-M, 3.OA.3). It would be impossible to teach this entire standard in one lesson. It is far too intricate and contains too many parts to do that. However, breaking this standard down into bite-sized daily objectives that in conjunction lead to students mastering it will be much more effective. (More on how to do that later in the chapter.)

Using the same broad standard for several days in a row can also lead to ineffective teaching. Providing specific, bite-sized objectives that change on a daily basis makes the teaching more strategic. (Lemov 2010, 61)

Clear

The clearer and more specific your learning objectives are, the more effectively you will be able to plan instruction. Vague objectives lead to vague teaching and lessons that potentially meander along a confusing path for students, rather than move them directly toward an outcome. Needless to say, this will not lead to student mastery. "Without a precise description of where they are headed, too many students are 'flying blind'" (Moss and Brookhart 2012, 2).

To make sure your objectives are clearly written, it helps to think about one question: "Is this objective written in a way that students would understand?" Student-friendly objectives, objectives that students can easily understand and make sense of, have language that students can read. "I can explicate a poem" is not a clear objective for a high-school English course because it's not only vague—what in the world is "explicate"—but it also contains language that students probably won't understand. A clearer objective might be "I can analyze the poet's use of figurative language."

This means that it is very important not to confuse objectives with activities. An example of this pitfall is an objective of "Students will complete 10 linear equation problems." Your objective must clearly state what students will learn how to do. Otherwise, students might equate learning with completing a task, rather than understanding information and building skills (Marzano 2011).

John Hattie's examination of more than 800 meta-analyses of student achievement research, detailed in his book *Visible Learning*, revealed "teacher clarity" as having one of the top 10 effect sizes on student achievement (Hattie 2012). Having clear learning objectives that can be effectively communicated to students in a way that they easily understand clearly falls into this category.

Aligned

Objectives should be written in a way that reflects an understanding of grade-level standards. As earlier stated, this does not mean that the daily learning objective should be the entire standard itself. Alignment is measured by asking: "Does this objective lead to the culmination of students' mastering of a standard?" When writing objectives, learning standards must be consulted. This will be explored in more depth later in the chapter, but now it's important to know exactly what this means.

An *aligned objective* is one that was written after consultation of the standards. Take for example a seventh-grade ELA teacher with an objective of "Students will be able to distinguish between first and third person narration in a story." On the outset, this seems to be an objective that is very strong. It can be measured, taught in one lesson, and it is clearly written. However, upon examination of the seventh-grade Common Core standard 7.RL.6, some alignment issues arise: "Analyze how an author develops and contrasts the points of view of different characters or narrators in a text." This objective does not appear to be aligned to the grade level standards, as it is focusing on specific types of points of view, rather than building toward an analysis of how an author develops or contrasts differing points of view. This objective is actually more suitably aligned to a *fourth-grade* reading standard, 4.RL.6: "Compare and contrast the point of view from which different stories are narrated, including the difference between first- and third-person narrations."

A Strong Objective Is

◆ **Measurable**—You can assess students' understanding of it following instruction.

◆ **Bite-sized**—It can be taught in a short amount of time, such as one class period.

◆ **Clear**—It is written in specific and student-friendly language.

◆ **Aligned**—It reflects attention to the language of grade-level standards.

Table 3.1 presents a collection of objectives that are missing one or more of these four traits, along with an explanation and a suggested improvement for each. At the end of the chapter, you will find an activity for practicing this on your own.

Table 3.1 Improving objectives

Objective	Explanation	Suggested Improvement
Students will be able to explore the cultures of East Asia. (Seventh Grade)	Exploration will be very difficult to measure. It also seems like a lot of content to cover in one lesson.	Students will be able to describe the cultural traditions of Japan.
Students will be able to add and subtract within 1,000 with and without regrouping. (Third Grade)	This objective is not bite-sized and needs to be broken down further into smaller objectives.	Students will be able to add two three-digit numbers.
Students will be able to read a sonnet. (Sixth Grade)	More specifics are needed. It is not clear what students will actually learn. In addition, this objective is difficult to measure.	Students will be able to describe the theme of a sonnet.
Students will be able to use place value understanding to round whole numbers to the nearest 10 or 100. (Second Grade)	Use of the phrase "place value understanding" might make this too unclear for students. Also, this aligns to a third-grade standard, not a second-grade standard.	Students will be able to round a number to the nearest 10. (Third Grade)

Building Objectives from Standards

Now that the qualities of an effective learning objective have been described, it is time to dig into where these objectives come from. Objectives should be built from broad goals that fully describe student mastery: learning standards. Standards serve as a guide from which we can work backwards. They lay out the end-of-year expectations, allowing teachers to construct a path by which to get there. This path is built from objectives.

This backwards design, begin-with-the-end-in-mind approach is not new. Described in detail in Grant Wiggins and Jay McTighe's 2005 book *Understanding by Design*, the process involves beginning the planning process by exploring the end outcomes first. In our case, we will begin with learning standards in mind.

Building objectives and lessons from standards is often referred to as "unpacking," but I find myself getting a little antsy when I hear that word—and I think a lot of teachers do, too. That's because many have been led to believe that unpacking standards is a daunting, challenging and time-consuming task best reserved for curriculum designers and experts. It is also a task that many believe has only one "right" way of being done.

To describe the process I prefer the word *unwrapping*, as coined by author and educator Larry Ainsworth (2004). Unwrapping has a much more pleasant connotation and is something that takes very little time. Unwrapping presents, unwrapping burritos . . . how fun! Unpacking after a trip? Not so much.

Regardless of what you call it, the purpose is the same—to examine a standard in order to determine what students need to know and do in order to master it, and thus what you need to teach them. With that purpose in mind, I will provide a description of things to think about when building objectives from standards, followed by examples of what this might look like in action. Remember, there is no one correct way to do this. You should customize and adapt this process to meet your individual preferences and the needs of your students.

Step 1: Read the Standard Closely

This may seem like a no-brainer, but it is such an important step that it must be mentioned. Only by reading the standard closely can we pull out the important details and key understandings that are mentioned within it. Since your goal is to identify what to teach and how to teach it, read the standard to look for important parts—specific verbs such as *analyze, describe,* and *compare*—as well as phrases like *real-world problems* and *within 1,000* that will help you direct your instruction. Some unpacking protocols guide teachers to pull out the verbs (skills) and nouns (knowledge) from a standard, so this might be useful to you, particularly in the next step.

Step 2: Identify Knowledge and Skills

Once you've read the standard carefully, it is time to ask the question "What do students have to know and be able to do in order to demonstrate mastery?" In other words, what will you have to help them understand? What will you have to teach them how to do? Make note of these things during this step and be sure to think about prior knowledge. This is also the time to identify skills and knowledge that students may have developed previously that play a role in this particular standard. There may be concepts, ideas, and abilities that aren't specifically mentioned in the standard, but that will be important for you to activate or touch upon to make sure students are prepared for the work that you are planning for them.

Step 3: Write Objectives

With the information in mind from Step 2, it's now time to break the knowledge and skills down into a list of objectives that are measurable, bite-sized, clear, and aligned. This collection of objectives represents all the things students will be able to do in order to master this standard. In essence, it represents what you have to teach. As or after you write the learning objectives, be sure to consider sequence—do these build upon one another and create a path toward mastery?

Building Objectives from Standards

1. Read the standard closely.
2. Identify knowledge and skills.
3. Write measurable, bite-sized, clear, and aligned objectives.

This process is similar to the one described in Chapter 2 about planning from assessments. The two could certainly be combined so that you are building objectives by examining *both* the assessment and the standard.

The following examples will be presented in a fashion that will hopefully provide more insight into what this process looks like in action. I'll put on my "teacher hat" and share what's on my mind as I work to build objectives from three different Common Core standards—one math, one writing, and one reading. Again, as a reminder, there is no one right way to do this. What I pull out might not necessarily match what you would pull out. It's the purpose that matters most—understanding the standards so as to create effective objectives.

Math Example

Standard 4.NF.2: <u>Compare two fractions with different numerators</u> and <u>different denominators</u>, e.g., by <u>creating common denominators or numerators</u>, or by <u>comparing to a benchmark fraction</u> such as 1/2. Recognize that <u>comparisons are valid only when the two fractions refer to the same whole</u>. Record the results of comparisons with <u>symbols >, =, or <</u>, and <u>justify the conclusions</u>, e.g., by using a <u>visual fraction model</u>.

Step 1—Read the Standard

During this step I want to be sure to pull out key phrases and ideas that can inform my planning. I've underlined these in the standard.

Step 2—Identify Knowledge and Skills

Students will have to know what a fraction represents, what denominators and numerators represent, what benchmark fractions are, that fractions can only be compared when they refer to the same whole, and the meaning of comparison symbols.

The skills this standard calls for include comparing two fractions, creating equivalent fractions by using common denominators or numerators, comparing fractions to a benchmark fraction, creating visual models of fractions, and justifying comparisons.

Step 3—Write Objectives

To master this standard, the following objectives will be taught:

- ◆ Students will be able to create equivalent fractions by creating common denominators and numerators.
- ◆ Students will be able to compare fractions using benchmark fractions.
- ◆ Students will be able to recognize that comparisons of fractions are valid only when they refer to the same whole.
- ◆ Students will be able to use <, >, and = to compare fractions.
- ◆ Students will be able to create visual models to compare two fractions.
- ◆ Students will be able to use a number line to compare two fractions.
- ◆ Students will be able to justify a comparison of fractions in writing.
- ◆ Students will be able to justify a comparison of fractions using visual models.
- ◆ Students will be able to justify a comparison of fractions using a number line.

A Note on the Common Core Math Standards

As noted in Chapter 1, there are some key instructional shifts that must be considered when examining the CCSS-M. One is that because the standards are linked in a coherent fashion within and across grades, it can be helpful to look at grade-level standards that are connected to the standard you are unpacking. In the case of this standard, 4.NF.2, it is helpful to examine the other standard in the "Extend understanding of fraction equivalence and ordering" cluster, 4.NF.1: "Explain, generate, and recognize equivalent fractions." It is highly likely that these two standards can be taught in conjunction, rather than in isolation, thereby maximizing instructional time and building student understanding in a more effective manner.

Furthermore, now is a good time to revisit the CCSS-M shift toward rigor—explained in Chapter 1 as a balance of conceptual understanding, procedural fluency, and application. It is helpful to check your objectives to make sure they reflect the aspects of rigor that are called for in the standard.

Writing Example

Standard W.7.1—Write arguments to support claims with clear reasons and relevant evidence.

W.7.1.A
Introduce claim(s), acknowledge alternate or opposing claims, and organize the reasons and evidence logically.

W.7.1.B
Support claim(s) with <u>logical reasoning</u> and <u>relevant evidence</u>, using <u>accurate, credible sources</u> and demonstrating an understanding of the topic or text.

W.7.1.C
<u>Use words, phrases, and clauses to create cohesion and clarify the relationships among claim(s), reasons, and evidence</u>.

W.7.1.D
Establish and maintain a <u>formal style</u>.

W.7.1.E
Provide a <u>concluding statement or section</u> that follows from and supports the argument presented.

Step 1—Read the Standard

Again, during this step I've underlined key words and phrases in the standard.

Step 2—Identify Knowledge and Skills

As I examine this standard, in my mind, I'm thinking that students need to know how to write an argumentative essay. Within this, they have to know what the following things are: a claim, an opposing claim, evidence, sources, and formal style.

The skills this standard calls for include writing an introduction, providing support for a claim, identifying sources, using linking or transition words and phrases, writing with a formal style, and writing in a logical, organized manner.

Step 3—Write Objectives

To master this standard, the following objectives will be taught:

◆ Students will be able to develop an argument or claim.
◆ Students will be able to identify and cite evidence that supports a claim.
◆ Students will be able to describe counter-arguments to a claim.
◆ Students will be able to write a paragraph that introduces their claim.

- ◆ Students will be able to distinguish between credible and non-credible sources.
- ◆ Students will be able to write clear paragraphs that are organized in a way that supports a claim.
- ◆ Students will be able to use transition words and phrases to connect paragraphs.
- ◆ Students will be able to recognize the difference between formal and informal writing styles.
- ◆ Students will be able to revise their writing to have a more formal style.
- ◆ Students will be able to write a conclusion paragraph that supports the claim they have presented.

Reading Example

Standard RL.5.2: <u>Determine a theme</u> of a story, drama, or poem <u>from details in the text</u>, including <u>how characters in a story or drama respond to challenges or how the speaker in a poem reflects upon a topic</u>; <u>summarize</u> the text.

Step 1—Read the Standard

This relatively short standard contains a great deal of information, as evidenced by the five key ideas underlined.

Step 2—Identify Knowledge and Skills

Knowledge and skills seem to blend together in this standard. Most importantly, in my mind, students will have to know what a theme is. They will also have to be able to describe the theme of a text and use details from the text to support their reasoning. Furthermore, they will have to understand that a theme is often revealed by how characters respond to challenges or by how a speaker describes something. Another important skill named here is the ability to summarize a text.

Step 3—Write Objectives

To master this standard, the following objectives will be taught:

- ◆ Students will be able to summarize a story, drama, or poem.
- ◆ Students will be able to describe the theme of a text.
- ◆ Students will be able to identify key details that support the theme of a text.
- ◆ Students will be able to describe the key challenges faced by a character in a story.

- Students will be able to explain how the challenges faced by characters help to reveal the theme of a story.
- Students will be able to describe the way a speaker discusses a topic in a poem.
- Students will be able to explain how the way a speaker discusses a topic in a poem reveals the theme of the poem.

A Note on the Common Core ELA Standards

Just as math standards should not be examined completely in isolation from other standards, the CCSS in ELA should not be examined in isolation from text. Incorporation of grade-level, complex text is at the foundation of the standards. So, for the writing example provided in this chapter, it would be important to think about what texts will be used to create an argument or claim. Selection of texts with rich themes would be crucial to the work around the reading example provided.

FAQ

My textbook provides me with objectives—can't I just use those?

You certainly can, but in order to increase the effectiveness of your lessons, it would be a good idea to conduct a quick audit of the objectives that are provided. Are they measurable, bite-sized, clear, and aligned? I would caution all teachers on being over-reliant on curricula. Use your professional judgement, and your knowledge of standards and best practice, to make solid instructional decisions. No one curriculum is perfect, particularly when it comes to the specific needs of your students. Examining curricula with a critical eye, rather than following along to the letter, will support your students in mastery of content.

Should each lesson have only one objective?

Having a single primary objective will help you keep things bite-sized. However, that does not mean that students will only develop their abilities around that single objective during your lesson. Other supporting concepts and skills might be combined to support the primary objective. The key is to make sure you are not trying to cover too much in one lesson, which will inhibit student mastery.

Is it important to phrase my objective in "student-friendly language?" I've been advised to do so.

When discussing the objective with students, it is important to be able to explain it in terms that they easily understand. (See Chapter 5 for more about explaining objectives to students during direct instruction.) In your plans, your objective doesn't necessarily have to be "student facing" (i.e., student friendly), but you should keep in mind that it's important for students to know what they are working on and why. Objectives become easier to master when students are able to understand them.

Why the need to spend so much time looking at standards?

Standards, no matter the grade or content area, represent the *what*—what students should know by the end of the school year. The more familiar you are with the standards, the better prepared your students will be for the next grade. It is a time-consuming process, but one that will better prepare you to plan effective lessons, lessons that drive students toward the understandings that will support their future learning and achievement.

My state does not use Common Core. What should I do to build objectives?

Regardless of which standards your state uses, the approach is the same. CCSS or not, you can unwrap any standard to develop objectives.

Activities

Activity 1: Assessing Objectives

Directions: Given an objective, analyze its effectiveness based upon the four criteria described in this chapter—measurable, bite-sized, clear, and aligned.

Objective	Explanation	Suggested Improvement
Students will be able to describe the differences between kinetic and potential energy as well as describe how one can be transferred into the other.		
Students will appreciate the genre of historical fiction.		
Students will be able to answer 10 square-root problems.		
Students will be able to apply the Pythagorean Theorem to multiple real-world scenarios in order to determine distances between points on and off a coordinate plane, given the lengths of two sides of right triangles.		
Students will know what it felt like to be a pioneer.		
Students will compare and contrast two texts.		
Students will understand the complexities of different governmental systems and different branches within those governments.		

Activity 2: Unwrapping Practice

Directions: Choose a standard you will teach in the near future. Unwrap it to determine the objectives you will teach.

Standard:	
Knowledge:	
Skills:	
Objectives:	

4

Writing Assessments

Learning is not attained by chance. It must be sought for with ardour and attended to with diligence.

—*Abigail Adams*

A strong objective in hand, it is now time for the second, and equally critical, "Before the Lesson" step: creating an end-of-lesson assessment. Your lesson's objective states *what* students will be able to do when the lesson is complete. The assessment determines *how* students will demonstrate mastery of the objective.

Often referred to as an *exit ticket, exit slip,* or *formative assessment,* the end-of-lesson assessment represents not only the measuring stick for the success of your lesson, but also the most critical resource for planning of the lesson itself. These assessments will be administered at the end of your lesson. However, creating a strong assessment *first,* before you even write your lesson plan, will allow you to begin with the end in mind and plan a lesson that leads to student understanding and mastery of the objective (Lemov 2010).

In this chapter, I will explore these types of assessments in depth, sharing important criteria and examples. The aim will be to provide an understanding of the important considerations that should be top-of-mind when beginning these steps. Surely, an exit slip is not the only means of assessing student understanding. Creating one is only the beginning. In subsequent chapters, I will detail other means of gathering information about student understanding during a lesson. Furthermore, in Chapter 8, you will read about what to do with the data you collect from these assessments.

Assessment Overview: Formative vs. Summative

Before digging into the creation of assessments, I am compelled to ground the work in *purpose* so that it is clear why these types of assessments are so important. There are several decades of research supporting the importance of formative assessment, which is assessment that informs instruction (Black and Wiliam 1998). However, I left college not really clear on the distinction between formative and summative assessments, let alone the value of the former. I think I understood summative assessments, but I was unclear on formative—which, naturally, led me to not implement them very effectively (or regularly) in my classroom.

The key to determining the difference lies in how the results of an assessment are used. Formative assessments are used to provide information during the instructional phase of the teaching and learning cycle, before a summative assessment is administered. Summative assessments are used to make a judgement about students—they are the unit tests and state assessments, for example, that come at the end, summing up what students are and aren't able to do (Chappius and Chappius 2008). See Table 4.1 for an overview of the two types of assessment.

As Black and his colleagues (2002) describe at the beginning of *Working Inside the Black Box*, a formative assessment is "any assessment for which the first priority in its design and practice is to serve the purpose of promoting pupils' learning. It thus differs from assessment designed primarily to serve the purposes of accountability, or of ranking, or of certifying competence."

Effective use of end-of-lesson formative assessments involves both carefully creating them and then using the results to make sound instructional decisions about what to do next and which students need which supports.

Table 4.1 Formative vs. summative assessments

Formative Assessments	Summative Assessments
Highlight the needs of each student	Compare all students to the same set of expectations
Provide immediate feedback	Provide feedback well after administration
Focus on progress or growth	Focus on a score, grade, or level
Inform immediate next steps	Describe overall mastery of content

Adapted from *Formative Assessment That Truly Informs Instruction* (NCTE Assessment Task Force, 2013).

They are a means of keeping your finger on the pulse of your class, and they have a proven effect on student achievement. According to John Hattie (2012) and his meta-analysis of educational research, formative evaluation is one of the top five influencers on student achievement. Furthermore, Black and Wiliam's (1998) research revealed that "improved formative assessment helps low achievers more than other students and so reduces the range of achievement while raising achievement overall" (3). So formative assessments not only increase student achievement, but they can have a significant impact on closing the achievement gap? Sign me up. Let's dig in!

Essentials of an End-of-Lesson Assessment

Just as with objectives, end-of-lesson assessments have a few essentials that should be considered when they are being created. End-of-lesson assessments should be brief, aligned, independent, and diagnostic. Here are the rationale for each.

Brief

These types of assessments should be short. You want students to be able to complete them in five minutes or less. Just as important, you want to be able to check them quickly as well. That way, you do not have to give up a large amount of class time to administration and you don't have to spend much time determining how to use the results to target students' misunderstandings. If either of these takes too long, you probably have too many questions on the assessment. It can be tempting to over-correct in this regard, though. Don't sacrifice quality data from student responses in your attempt to be brief. For example, asking students for a thumbs-up or thumbs-down in response to a question at the end of the lesson won't provide effective formative data. Yes, it's brief, but students might be influenced by classmates, thus invalidating the data.

Aligned

In the case of formative assessments, it is critical that they are aligned to the objective. In other words, the answer to the question "Does this assessment reflect what I want students to be able to do?" should be "Yes." A common pitfall is for assessments to assess more than the objective calls for. The objective names what you plan to teach, so the assessment should only assess that. The content and rigor of the assessment must align to the content and rigor of the objective. It isn't the time for building in review, or pushing students to go beyond what you taught. Those things do have value, but can be done at other times. You want your assessments to be laser-focused on what your objective names as the learning target for the lesson. Before digging into the planning of the lesson and the student work, it's a great idea to hold the objective and assessment side-by-side to be sure they line up and that both will drive students' learning to the same place.

Independent

Students should complete the exit assessment on their own, rather in groups. That way you can identify the needs and strengths of every individual in your classroom. Collaborative work has its place and is an effective strategy for many lessons. However, it isn't an effective means of gathering data about individual students. Whatever the makeup of your end-of-lesson assessment, students should complete it on their own.

Diagnostic

Remember, the purpose of this assessment is to diagnose students' understanding. You want to be able to learn about what they know from their work. This requires careful planning because you have to craft the assessment while giving thought to what information it is going to give you. Is it going to show you what they know and don't know? What they understand and don't understand? That is clearly your goal and should be kept in mind when designing the assessment. For example, if your exit ticket is made up of one or more multiple choice questions (many teachers use "clickers" or other student-response systems for this type of assessment), you will want to create incorrect choices that make sense and reveal students' thinking. If you're teaching a math lesson, having students show their work will help you make more informed instructional decisions. In any subject, if you are asking students to explain themselves in writing, being as specific as possible when asking them what to write about will help with these decisions, as well.

End-of-Lesson Assessment Essentials

◆ *Brief*—It should not take long to administer or evaluate.
◆ *Aligned*—It should be designed with the objective in mind.
◆ *Independent*—Students should complete the assessment on their own
◆ *Diagnostic*—The assessment should reveal students' misunderstandings

Building an End-of-Lesson Assessment

Keeping these essentials in mind, you can set about creating your assessment. The following suggestions can help you build an exit ticket that will allow you to obtain invaluable information—which students understand your objective, which ones do not, and why.

Utilize Your Objective

When crafting an assessment for students to complete at the end of your lesson, it's important to work alongside the objective. Remember, it is the objective that describes exactly what you want students to do. The exit ticket and objective should work hand-in-hand. Be sure that nothing is on your assessment that isn't described in the objective. For example, if the objective is "Students will be able to multiply 3 digit numbers by 2 digit numbers using the standard algorithm," you will want to make sure that your assessment contains only 3-by-2 multiplication. And since the objective makes no mention of word problems, you would also want to make sure your assessment doesn't feature this type of work. (Of course if you are really teaching word problems, then you should adjust your objective.)

The verb you use in your objective can be a useful guide when it comes to creating your assessment. Your assessment should reflect this verb. If you want students to "describe" or "evaluate," or "justify," then the exit slip should call for students to do these things.

Consider Rigor Cognitive Demand

The often-used term *rigor* remains a fairly mysterious term for educators. I've come to prefer the phrase *cognitive demand*, because that seems to more accurately describe this very important idea. When I think about my assessment, it's important to consider the cognitive demand, or depth of thinking, that I will expect of students. In many cases, it may be helpful to pull back from looking at an individual objective to examination of your sequence of objectives. Do they build from lower cognitive demand to higher? If so, your assessments should build in this way, too. If you're working on a concept that requires starting from a fundamental level and moving deeper into the complexities of a topic, your assessments in the initial lessons will be different from your assessments in the final lessons.

Consider a sixth-grade ELA teacher, working with standard RL.6.4: *Determine the meaning of words and phrases as they are used in a text, including figurative and connotative meanings; analyze the impact of a specific word choice on meaning and tone.* Initial lessons might work with developing students' understanding of figurative and connotative language. As their work with this standard progresses, word choice will be something they explore, specifically the impact words have on meaning and tone. Ideally, the teacher will want to tie all these things together. The assessments for this sequence should reflect this progression.

In keeping with the desire to keep your assessment brief, it's important to remember that, as Barbara Blackburn writes in *Rigor is NOT a Four-Letter Word*, rigor does not mean "more" (2012, 3). Avoid asking 10 questions when three (or fewer) will suffice. Asking students to explain, justify, or support their answer in writing or asking questions that require multiple steps is a much more effective means of increasing the cognitive demand than simply adding more of the same type of question to your assessment. Again, just be sure that the assessment aligns to the objective (i.e. if your exit ticket requires explanation or multiple steps, your objective should clearly state that).

Create Exemplar Answers

When creating your end-of-lesson assessments, a key step is to create exemplar answers to your assessment items. An exemplar answer defines and clarifies your expectations for student work. This standard of excellence will aid you in determining which students have mastered the objective. It will also help inform your planning, so that you know exactly where you want students to get to by the end of your lesson.

A Note on Small Groups

Many teachers differentiate instruction by working in small groups. The end-of-lesson assessments that have been discussed in this chapter apply, in general, to whole-group instruction. However, they can also be utilized in small groups, where the objectives might differ from that of the whole-group lesson. It can be effective and beneficial to assess the small-group work as well, so that you can determine the students' understandings in these differentiated situations.

FAQ

What if none (or very few) of my students demonstrate mastery on their exit slips?

This is an incredibly important question, and one that we will examine in more detail in Chapter 8. In essence, if your exit slip is well-designed and aligns to your objective, it means that students do not understand what you taught them and reteaching will be necessary. Many things should be taken into consideration to determine the causes of misunderstanding, and those will be explored in Chapter 8.

My curriculum provides end-of-lesson assessments, should I use those?

These assessments might be very useful. However, it's crucial that you audit them before putting them in front of students. Do they actually align with the objective that you're teaching? Do they assess only the content you will be delivering and not anything extra or superfluous? Is anything missing from them? Do they meet the four essentials described in this chapter? As discussed in Chapter 3, an overreliance on a curriculum can often impede student mastery. So, of course, you should use them, but not blindly nor without examining them carefully.

Why should my assessment be made first?

Paired with a strong objective, an assessment can serve as a road map for your planning. By beginning with the outcomes you want students to achieve, you can plan more effectively for them to get there. Think of it in the same way as planning a vacation. It is much more simple to know your destination before you start planning activities and booking flights and hotels. When you start at Point A and you know where Point B is, you can more effectively plan how to move from one to the other in a way that allows for students to succeed.

Activity 1: Evaluating Assessments

Directions: The following table presents several objectives and end-of-lesson assessments. For each assessment, determine how it should be revised. Keep in mind the assessment essentials described in this chapter: *Brief, Aligned, Independent,* and *Diagnostic.*

Objective	Assessment	Revision
Students will be able to solve word problems with two-digit by one-digit multiplication.	Solve: There are 28 students. Each brings three boxes of pencils. Each box has 12 pencils. How many pencils were brought in in all?	
Students will compare and contrast how two characters in a story changed.	What changed about Jarvis in the story? a. He got braver. b. He became stronger. c. He learned new things. What changed about James in the story? a. He learned a new skill. b. He became nicer. c. He changed his mind about Jarvis.	
Students will be able to identify allusions in a text.	Write a paragraph about why the author may have chosen to include this allusion in the story. Cite specific evidence from the text to support your answer.	
Students will use the distributive property to solve expressions.	In your own words, describe the distributive property.	

Activity 2: Design an End-of-Lesson Assessment

Choose an objective you created in Chapter 3 and create an end-of-lesson assessment that matches the requirements outlined in this chapter.

Standard:	
Objective:	
End-of-Lesson Assessment:	

Part III
During the Lesson

5

Direct Instruction

If you can't explain it simply, you don't understand it well enough.
—*Albert Einstein*

In this section, I describe the lesson-planning process in full. Moving from designing objectives and assessment prior to the lesson, we will now discuss the planning of the lesson itself.

I'll begin with an overview of this planning model as a whole. It is grounded in the model of gradual release of responsibility, a framework in which the workload shifts over the course of time from the instructor to the student (Fisher and Frey 2008, 2). While this can take many different iterations (which will be discussed along the way), this will take the form of a lesson plan with three parts: direct instruction, guided practice, and independent practice (often referred to as *I do, we do, you do*). Each will be described in detail in the following three chapters. Combined with an effective objective and a quality end-of-lesson assessment, these three lesson portions work together in a cohesive manner to create a lesson designed to lead to student mastery of content.

It is my goal to provide details and examples in an easy-to-understand format as well as in a way that will allow you to implement this planning framework the very next time you sit down to plan lessons. It is certainly a rigorous process and one that requires a great deal of thought, energy, and time. But the outcome—student achievement—makes all this worth it. Like so many things, lesson planning becomes easier and more efficient with practice. You may initially find yourself spending a great deal of time on planning. But perseverance and patience will be rewarded, and you will notice the process taking less time the more often you use it.

Direct Instruction: An Overview

So let's begin with direct instruction, the beginning portion of the lesson plan. Often called the "I do" or mini-lesson, it involves the teacher as the centerpiece, modeling, thinking aloud, and demonstrating and activating thinking and curiosity (Zemelman, Daniels and Hyde 2012, 40). Direct instruction should not be confused with lecturing. A lecture is lengthy and does not lead to any sort of student activity other than note taking. Yes, for the most part, direct instruction involves the teacher doing the work and the talking while students listen, but it should be brief. It should last no longer than 10 to 15 minutes—and of course it will be followed by students engaging in the lesson.

The beginning of your lesson is of critical importance. There are many goals to achieve in the first few minutes: capturing students' attention, connecting to prior work, communicating the lesson's objective and its purpose, demonstrating for students how to do the work, and confirming students' readiness to begin the work. That's a lot to accomplish in a short amount of time!

Goals of Direct Instruction

- ◆ Capturing students' attention
- ◆ Connecting to prior work
- ◆ Communicating the objective and its purpose
- ◆ Demonstrating the "how"
- ◆ Confirming readiness to begin the work

We will dig into each of these in a moment, but first a bit about purpose . . . why is direct instruction important? As a teacher—and I've certainly done this in my own classroom many times—it's natural to want to get students "involved" as soon as possible. The idea of them sitting and listening and watching you talk and do the work is a bit terrifying. What if they get bored? What if they're not listening? What if they don't understand? Valid questions, but ones that can be handled with a well-planned opening.

Remember, this portion of the lesson should be no more than 10 minutes. In some cases, especially in younger grades, it could be as short as five minutes. This should alleviate some of the pressure to keep students focused and "entertained." Less is more during direct instruction, and clarity is of utmost importance.

Does Direct Instruction Have to Happen First?

As you read this book, it is important to keep in mind that there is never a one-size-fits-all approach to planning. Case in point: direct instruction. Not every lesson has to start in the way I've described. All of the essentials of direct instruction are important, but there are times when lessons should begin in other ways.

Many teachers will utilize a beginning-of-lesson activity to engage students in the work right away. Sometimes called a "Do Now," this activity can take the form of a single question or problem that serves to activate students' thinking or prior knowledge. Sometimes, this activity can serve as a sort of preassessment to determine exactly what students are bringing to the work. Other times, it can be helpful to begin with a challenging task or problem, one that is just out of students' reach but that can be helpful for stimulating student discussion and collaboration.

However you begin your lesson, and in whichever way you choose to order these essentials, keeping them in mind will aid your planning as you make instructional decisions based upon your students' needs.

Teacher and Student Roles During Direct Instruction

During this portion of the lesson, the teacher is doing almost all of the work. The responsibility for the thinking must fall on the teacher's shoulders in the beginning of the lesson. Only that way can it be gradually shifted onto the students. To assist in providing clarity around this, it is important to consider what both the teacher and the student should be doing during this (and all) parts of the lesson (Lemov 2010).

The Teacher's Role
This mini-lesson time is for the teacher to be modeling, thinking aloud, wondering, and demonstrating. It is an opportunity for the teacher to let the students see into his or her brain to help them better understand the concepts

they will begin working on. Furthermore, direct instruction allows for the instructor to develop students' metacognition, teaching them how to think about their own thinking, not only during this lesson but during every other task or problem they will encounter (Fisher and Frey 2008).

For all of this to get started, it will be the teacher doing almost all of the talking—and this talking should be declarative, rather than interrogatory. This is your opportunity to explain things to students, not a time to ask them questions. Too often, teachers want to jump in to ask students questions about how to solve a problem or complete a task before they have explained how to do it. But how can a student be expected to explain how to do something new when they haven't been shown how yet? You can ask me what the first step in repairing a lawn mower engine is, but I'm not going to know the answer unless you show me what to do first.

So if the teacher is solely driving the lesson at this point, what should he or she be saying? Keep the outcome of direct instruction in mind: preparing students to start doing the work. Your direct instruction should provide them with all the necessary tools they need to begin the work. Two techniques that many teachers use successfully during direct instruction are modeling and thinking aloud. As you will see when we explore some examples of direct instruction plans, the two are ideally interwoven. For clarity's sake, though, we will explore them individually.

A Note on Clarity

The quote from Albert Einstein that I shared at the beginning of this chapter is not one that I chose accidentally: "If you can't explain it simply, you don't understand it well enough."

When thinking about the teacher's role during direct instruction, it is of the utmost importance to remember to keep your explanations, thoughts, and examples as clear as possible. During planning, you should nag yourself with the question, "Will my students understand this?" If you're worried that they won't, take Albert's advice and learn more about what you're teaching, either through research or conversations with colleagues. That way simplicity and clarity will shine through, and your students will reap the benefits.

Modeling

To model is to demonstrate, to show how to solve a problem, answer a question, or complete a task. When you model, you take on the role of the student in that *you* are the one doing the work. Modeling should be explicit, deliberate, and clear. Every step should be demonstrated, no matter how minute. You want students to begin the next phase of the lesson, guided practice, with a very clear idea of how to do the day's work.

Thinking Aloud

Just modeling alone isn't enough. Modeling without thinking aloud is like watching a movie without sound. It's tough to understand what's going on without narration! Thinking aloud does just that, it provides narration to the work, so that students are thinking about what they should be thinking about, rather than just what they should do. Thinking aloud should go beyond telling, though. It should involve explaining. (Fisher and Frey 2008, 18) Explaining involves sharing all of your thinking—the questions you're asking yourself, the pitfalls you're avoiding, the connections and decisions you are making, and any other relevant thoughts that will help ensure students are ready to take on the work themselves.

Variations on the Think-Aloud

In *Best Practice: Bringing Standards to Life in America's Classrooms*, Zemelman, Daniels, and Hyde (2012) present two variations on the think-aloud—the write-aloud and the search-aloud (pp. 44–45). These options are worthy of consideration, as they may fit the specifics of your individual lessons in various subjects.

A **write-aloud** involves the teacher demonstrating his or her thinking while composing a piece of writing. This allows students to better understand the thought processes required for written work.

A **search-aloud** fits nicely into lessons about research or whenever combing through a text to locate information is required. In this variation, the teacher shares their thinking while he or she searches, narrating the process so that students will be prepared to do the same on their own, whether for a research assignment or project involving the Internet, or for a lesson involving a close reading of a text.

The Student's Role

While direct instruction involves the teacher doing the thinking, working, and explaining, it is important to consider the students' role, too. Active listening is their most important responsibility. In my experiences, this works best when students are *not* taking notes, answering questions, or reading aloud. Their work here involves following along and thinking about what it is you are showing and explaining. It's that simple—but calling on students for answers during direct instruction is an easy trap to fall into. Resist it so that the responsibility for the work lies with you.

At the conclusion of the direct instruction, checking for understanding is important, and this is where students become more actively involved. This allows the teacher to make sure that students are ready to move on to guided practice.

Essentials of Direct Instruction

With the basics under our belts, it's now time to explore the essential elements of direct instruction in more detail. The goal here is to orient you to how to plan for this brief, yet important, part of the lesson. Of course, you should tailor these essentials to your own needs and the needs of your students. The specifics of your lesson will also help you determine what role these essentials play and in what order you present them, especially the first three. As with everything in this book, be sure to make it work for you.

That being said, these six elements can set you up for success in the later part of your lesson. Let's take an in-depth look at each.

Alignment to the Objective and Assessment
Alignment is a topic I will stress throughout this book. When I use the term "alignment," what I'm talking about is a logical connection between the lesson's parts. In the case of direct instruction, there should be alignment to the objective and end-of-lesson assessment.

In other words, a clear and logical connection should be able to be made between the lesson objective and the direct instruction.

Capturing Students' Attention
This might sound more intimidating than it should be. Capturing students' attention is something that I'm sure entire books could be written about. But for your direct instruction, anything simple will do. Maybe this involves telling a story about a recent experience, sharing a problem, showing a (very) short video, or sharing an anecdote from prior classes you've taught. A big goal of direct instruction is activating students' thinking, and this can be where it begins.

Some notes of caution, however—keep your time frame in mind. Fifteen minutes is the absolute longest you want this mini-lesson to last. If you tell a story for 10 minutes, that doesn't leave enough time for modeling and thinking aloud! Also, don't put pressure on yourself to be overly humorous or exciting. I say both of these things because I fashion myself to be an excellent storyteller and a hilarious person, but I have a tendency to be a little long-winded and overzealous when trying to capture my students' attention. You know your students better than me, so just plan this element carefully to be simple and brief and you're sure to be successful.

Connecting to Prior Work

In many cases, it is possible to activate students' thinking about prior work during direct instruction. This can be very helpful when teaching lessons that build upon work students have done before, whether earlier in the school year or in previous grades. Reminding them about this knowledge not only gets them actively thinking as you work, but it enables them to see how so many academic concepts and instructional activities are connected. This helps them realize that their learning is not taking place in isolation, but rather as a series of interrelated concepts and ideas that link together to create meaning and understanding.

Like capturing their attention, this can and should be done briefly. Depending upon your objective, you may only need a sentence or two. "Remember how we looked at the parts of stories last month?" or "This connects to the work we did with absolute value because . . ." This simple step goes a long way toward constructing meaning and deepening understanding, as well as toward students' mastery of your objective.

Communicating the Objective and Its Purpose

Making it clear what students will be learning is important. This can be done by explaining your learning objective at the beginning of the lesson. Doing so in a way that students can easily understand will create a frame around which they will build understanding. You should go beyond just writing your objective on the board and expecting students to grasp its meaning (Marzano 2011).

Equally as important is the communication of why students will be doing the work of the lesson. Explaining its relevance and its role in the bigger picture of their learning can help them assign value to the work. Think about it, as a learner yourself reading this book, the emphasis I've placed upon purpose has hopefully added relevance. The lessons and content you present to students are important. You believe this, to be sure. Otherwise, you would not spend valuable time preparing and presenting the lessons that you do. However, do your students understand the importance and the purpose of the material you are delivering and the activities you are engaging them in? If not, their investment and interest will decrease. As Fisher and Frey write in *The Purposeful Classroom*, "A lack of purpose can devolve into low-level measurement of compliance and assignment completion, rather than learn-ing" (2011, 15–16).

Demonstrating the "How"

This is where the modeling and thinking aloud comes in. Since I've already covered a description of this process of teacher-directed instruction earlier in this chapter, here I will explain how this comes to life in your lesson plans. Knowing what modeling, explaining, and thinking aloud are is one thing; it is quite another to understand how to plan them.

When planning for this portion of the lesson, where you are doing the work, it is important to plan three things: what you will say (think-alouds), what you will show (modeling), and what potential errors and misconcep-tions you want to address.

Addressing Major Misconceptions

Direct instruction provides an opportunity to engage students in thinking about where things might possibly go wrong. As you begin to plan any les-son, potential pitfalls for students should be at the forefront of your mind. Use your content expertise to help you predict where students might have trouble so that you can address these misunderstandings *before they happen.* One option is to explicitly mention these types of errors during direct instruc-tion. Because teachers can foresee many of the most common errors, this can be a very effective way of bringing these mistakes to students' attention before they have the opportunity to make them. Making notes on possible misconceptions as you plan will help you remember to include them during direct instruction.

Confirming Readiness to Begin the Work

This portion of the direct instruction serves a very important purpose. After you have modeled, demonstrated, and shared your thinking with students, you will need to check to make sure that they are ready to move on to the next phase, guided practice. This checkpoint will allow you to make sure that they have understood and internalized the content that you have shared with them and that they now are able to be gradually released to take on a slight bit more of the workload.

When planning your direct instruction, consider what you want to ask students or have them do that will indicate an understanding of what you've taught thus far. Write this question into your plans, as well as what you would expect their answer to be. Planning this out in advance will allow you to ascertain their understanding and determine if you should move on or circle back for more direct instruction. In circling back, you may have to

Figure 5.1 Check for Understanding flow chart

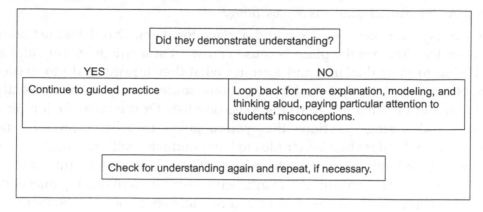

model another problem or think aloud more thoroughly. At this point, it will also be critical to address misunderstandings that were revealed by the students' answers.

Checkpoints like this, often called *checks for understanding*, should be present throughout your lesson (they will be discussed in more depth in Chapter 6), so this will be the first of several. But as the first one, it certainly carries a heightened level of importance.

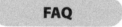

FAQ

How long should direct instruction last?

Direct instruction is sometimes referred to as a mini-lesson, with an emphasis on *mini*. It is something that should only take 5–10 minutes. If it takes longer than this, you might be trying to teach too much. You may need to revisit objective and revise it to be more bite-sized.

Direct instruction sounds a lot like lecture. Isn't that a bad thing?

Delivering instruction via lecture—wherein the teacher talks for oftentimes an entire class period while students are expected to take notes—is certainly not an effective means to engage students in a meaningful way. Like lecturing, direct instruction does involve the teacher talking while students listen. However, direct instruction lasts for only a fraction of the class period. Furthermore, direct instruction calls upon the teacher to *show* students what to do and how to do it rather than *telling* students what to do and how to do it, as often is the case during lectures.

My students like to ask questions when I'm modeling at the beginning of my lessons. Aren't student questions a good thing?

Absolutely! But there is a time and a place for them. Direct instruction is neither the time nor the place because you want students following along, listening to your thinking, and learning what they'll need to do to master the objective of the day. By asking questions, students may be inadvertently missing out on what you're trying to accomplish. Or they may be jumping ahead and asking questions that you're going to answer later in the mini-lesson. It might be a better idea to have students wait until you're done modeling and thinking aloud to ask questions. You also might want to examine and reflect on your direct instruction—are students asking questions because you're not being as clear as you possibly could be? Maybe there are adjustments you could make that would make it easier for students to follow along and understand.

Activity: Planning Direct Instruction

Use this template to write a direct instruction plan for an objective you created in Chapter 3. Be sure to include potential student misunderstandings, as these will guide your planning in every phase.

Objective:
Potential student misunderstandings:
Direct instruction: *Modeling:*   *Think-alouds:*   *Check for understanding:*

6

Guided Practice

Education is all a matter of building bridges.

—*Ralph Ellison*

With a strong plan for direct instruction in place, you are now ready to plan the next part of your lesson: guided practice. In my experience as both a teacher and instructional coach, this section of the lesson can be challenging to execute. Guided practice brings the students into the lesson, actively engaging them in the work for the first time. Many pieces are put into motion, some of them at the same time. This requires intentional and thoughtful planning, in order to be sure that your lesson stays on track.

Before digging into the essentials of guided practice, it is important to understand the thinking behind this lesson element, which is grounded in some very important educational research.

Guided Practice—An Overview (Understanding Gradual Release of Responsibility)

Guided practice is built upon the work of several educational researchers and is driven by the model of gradual release of responsibility, developed by P. David Pearson and Meg Gallagher in 1983. In this section of the lesson, the responsibility of thinking and working is shifted from the teacher—the one doing the thinking and working during direct instruction—to students.

The goal is to gradually call upon students to do more over the course of the guided practice so that they are ready to do the work on their own during independent practice. In essence, this model "assumes that [the student] will need some guidance in reaching that stage of independence and that is precisely the teacher's role to provide such guidance" (Pearson and Gallagher, 1983, 35).

This model is supported by the work of psychologist Lev Vygotsky, who described a "zone of proximal development." Within this zone are the skills that students can complete only with the assistance of an adult or peer, whom Vygotsky calls a "more knowledgeable other" (Vygotsky 1978, 86). The Gradual Release model also aligns with the concept of "scaffolding," which is a term familiar to many educators. Wood and Middleton (1975) compare instructional support to scaffolding that is put up to support a building. Teachers provide the support needed for students to develop understanding, and then remove that support one piece at a time until the building can stand on its own. (Wood, Bruner, and Ross 1976)

One common way of describing a gradual release lesson is: *I do it* (direct instruction), *we do it* (guided practice), *you do it* (independent practice). However, it isn't exactly that simple. Direct instruction (described in Chapter 5) and independent practice (Chapter 7) are straightforward in that the responsibility and cognitive load rests for the most part with one group in each—the teacher during direct instruction and the learner during independent practice. During guided practice, the responsibility shifts incrementally and intentionally, bridging the gap between the first and third parts of the lesson in a way that adequately prepares students to handle the work or task on their own. Figures 6.1 and 6.2 illustrate the way the responsibility shifts over time.

Figure 6.1 Teacher responsibility during the lesson

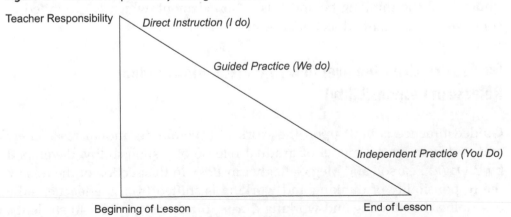

Figure 6.2 Student responsibility during the lesson

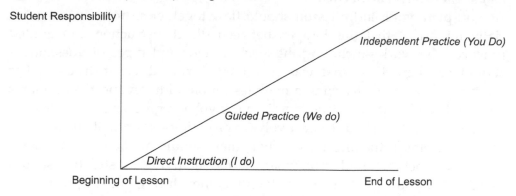

Think about a time you learned how to do something. Regardless if it was learning how to use a new cell phone or change the headlight in your car, you might have taught yourself or had someone show you. If you had to do the same thing again, could you do it without help? If the responsibility of the work was not gradually released to you (i.e. the cell phone company support desk told you exactly what to do, or you read a manual on your own, or you tinkered around until you figured it out), you are far less likely to be able to have mastered the task such that you could complete it again or even teach it to someone else. These examples aren't perfectly aligned to the work of classroom teaching, but the connection is clear. True understanding and mastery is much more likely to occur when the Gradual Release model is used.

Understanding the fundamentals, purpose, and goals of Gradual Release of Responsibility is critical to developing a strong lesson plan, and particularly important for planning guided practice. When guided practice is not planned to match this gradual release, students either end up doing too much of the work without enough support or teachers end up doing too much of the work (think: lecturing) without preparing the students to work independently. This portion of the lesson requires skillful planning, which will lead to deft execution. This, in turn, will lead to more successful outcomes in regards to student achievement and mastery.

Essentials of Guided Practice

There are several keys to strong guided practice. Some of them—such as whole and small group work, and engaging discussion—overlap. Guided practice can certainly look different in different classrooms. However, consider these essentials as you plan.

Alignment to Direct Instruction

As you plan, your entire lesson should flow together seamlessly. It's especially important that this happen between direct instruction and guided practice. The work—including the level of rigor and types of questions—should be aligned to what was presented during direct instruction. For example, if you were teaching a math lesson on addition and the problems you modeled in direct instruction did not involve regrouping, the problems in guided practice should not involve regrouping either. If there were no word problems in the direct instruction, there should not be word problems in guided practice. Simply put, what you model in direct instruction should match what you and students work on together during guided practice.

Lack of alignment is a pitfall for many lessons. This is especially true when teachers are over-reliant on a particular curriculum. Even textbooks that seem to follow a gradual release approach often aren't aligned from one part of the lesson to the next. This can throw off a lesson and lead to poor performance on the end-of-lesson assessment. Alignment should be at the top of your mind when planning guided practice. Pay careful attention to the work you are asking students to do during this section, especially if you are planning from curricular resources. Assessing your alignment as you plan is a relatively simple step that can yield tremendous results for your students.

Whole-Group Work

You can think of your guided practice as having two parts. The first is whole-group work. During this time, the entire class engages in the work together. This involves the teacher presenting a problem, question, or situation while the class works together as a whole to solve or answer. It provides an opportunity to leverage the thinking of the group, as you can call on students to share their thinking and ask probing questions to check for understanding.

Gradual release should be evident during whole-group work, as well. For example you might start by solving a problem or discussing a question as a whole class and then move to working on a different question in pairs or small groups, with groups sharing their answers and their thinking to the whole class when they are done.

Small-Group Work

The second part of guided practice should involve students working in collaborative groups. Whole-group work can transfer very easily into small-group work, as you see in the earlier description. The importance of providing students with the time and space to work collaboratively cannot be emphasized enough. In fact in determining which part of guided practice to prioritize, you should usually select small-group work. This is the phase where "students consolidate their thinking and understanding. Negotiating with peers, discussing ideas and information, or engaging in inquiry with others causes students to use what they learned" in whole-group work and direct instruction (Fisher and Frey 2008).

This small-group work can take many forms, from working on a math problem together to a shared reading of a text. The key is that the work is shared and that students are empowered to engage in discussion with one another. During collaborative discussions, students are able to receive feedback and support from their peers in a much more extensive fashion than they can receive from a single teacher (Zemelman, Daniels, and Hyde 2012).

Research supports the theory that collaborative learning has a positive impact upon student achievement. Vygotsky (1978) reported that students are able to perform at higher levels of intellect when working and discussing with other students. Johnson and Johnson (1986) and Webb (1985) also have done extensive work exploring the benefits of collaborative work, finding that there is a link between student interaction and achievement.

Engaging Discussion

An oft-overlooked element of any lesson is the discussion. Engaging discussion should be embedded into both whole-group and small-group work. The conversations that the students have during guided practice will generate thinking and understanding that is invaluable in their progress toward mastering the lesson's objective. The key is that the discussion is structured so that everyone is involved.

While there is a time and place for a teacher asking questions and calling on students for answers, particularly during whole-group work, there is greater value in setting up a discussion such that every student is able to engage in a conversation about a problem or question. This can be done very easily by allowing students to discuss your questions in pairs or small groups. Often called a turn-and-talk or think-pair-share, where students discuss with a partner, this strategy allows every student to engage in the discussion.

A Note on Thinking Aloud

In discussions that take place during guided practice, as in direct instruction, the teacher continues to share his or her thoughts using think alouds. (See Chapter 5 for more on think-alouds.)

However, in guided instruction, seize the opportunity for *students* to become the ones that share their thinking. When students think aloud, they provide insight into not only their thought processes, but to the way they are engaging in the learning (Fisher and Frey 2008). This can go beyond providing you, the teacher, with a window into their minds, but it can do the same for their fellow students. This can prove invaluable, as students are able to process the thinking of not only the teacher, but of their fellow classmates as well.

During guided practice, push students to share their thinking aloud. Every student will benefit from this.

But how do you know students are discussing the right things? As *Teach Like a Champion* author Doug Lemov writes, effectively executed turn-and-talks definitely get students discussing, but that doesn't mean they are without pitfalls. With every student talking with a partner, these discussions cannot be completely monitored by the teacher. This opens the door for students to come up with incorrect answers or unsubstantiated opinions. The best way to avoid this, Lemov (2014) writes on the *Teach Like a Champion* blog, "is to pair the turn-and-talk with a subsequent activity that allows you to reinforce rigor and check for understanding." He recommends bringing the ideas to the group for a reflective and analytical group discussion, perhaps cueing it up with a statement such as: "Let's look at what we came up with and see what makes the most sense . . . where we could add on."

Checking for Understanding

At this point of your lesson, it is critical that you determine whether or not students are ready to work independently at mastering the objective. The reflection described earlier can serve as a checkpoint for you to check the pulse of your students' understanding. It can also help you to determine who might need more support during the remainder of the lesson, both of which are essentials of a strong check for understanding.

You may encounter three scenarios when checking for understanding at the end of guided practice: the entire class understands, a majority of the class does not understand, or some students understand and some do not. If the entire class is ready for independent practice, congratulations! Your hard work paid off; it's time for independent practice. But if either the entire class is still struggling or you have a handful of students that are not demonstrating understanding, you either need to loop back and extend guided practice for the entire class or target individual students for immediate intervention as soon as independent practice begins, as Figure 6.3 shows.

Figure 6.3 Student responsibility during the lesson

Did students demonstrate understanding?		
YES	NO (whole group)	NO (individuals)
Continue to independent practice	Extend guided practice by looping back for more collaborative work or discussion, then check for understanding again.	Move whole group to independent practice but check-in with individuals or small groups immediately to eliminate misconceptions.

Remember, your main goal in checking for understanding is to assess *individual* student readiness. The reflections from a group discussion may not reflect individual understanding, as they may have been generated or supported by a classmate. That's not to say that this data isn't valuable—you can still learn a great deal from what students share out following small-group work. Therefore it is important to gauge student understanding at an individual level before moving on in your lesson. Some teachers do this by asking students to answer a question on their own while they work the room to examine papers. Others do it by having students write their answers on small whiteboards and then hold them up for the teacher to see. Regardless of the technique you use, be as confident as you can in your assessment of each students' readiness for the individual work that he or she will be called on to complete during independent practice.

Essentials of Guided Practice

- ◆ Alignment to direct instruction
- ◆ Whole-group work
- ◆ Small-group work
- ◆ Engaging discussion
- ◆ Checking for understanding

Teacher and Student Roles During Guided Practice

As you have learned, during guided practice the work and the cognitive load shifts from teacher to students. In your planning of guided practice, the roles of both teacher and student should be considered. To help you better understand what each of these might look like, I'll provide some elaboration.

Teacher's Role

The most important part for the teacher to remember, of course, is that the responsibility is gradually being released to students. There are some other things to keep in mind, as well.

Evidence Gathering

While students are working in both whole and small groups, you should be continually gathering evidence of student understanding. Whether by making note of students' answers or by circulating amongst small groups to listen in and examine their work, you are seeking one thing: proof that students are understanding the objective in such a way that they will be ready to work independently. The more effort you put into evidence gathering, the more confident you can be about students' readiness. You should gather evidence in a way that allows you to be certain about exactly which students are ready and which need more support. Interventions can take place on-the-fly as you touch base with small groups or they may need to occur on a one-on-one basis during independent practice. Either way, your investigative work and evidence gathering should occur throughout guided practice.

Effective Questioning

Whether during whole-group or small-group work, the questions you ask should work to deepen student understanding and to create an environment for engaging discussion. In some cases, this will require you to script in advance the questions you want to ask. In other instances, having a set of "universal prompts" can benefit you tremendously (Bambrick-Santoyo, Settles, and Worrell 2013). These can include questions such as "Why do you think that?" or "What makes you think that?" or "What were you thinking about when you came up with that?" Even a simple "Tell me more" can go a long way toward pushing students to think more critically about their answers.

Flexibility

This may be a statement of the obvious, but your lesson plan is just that—a plan. Those of us who have spent more than five minutes in a classroom know that what they say about the best-laid plans is 100 percent true! But during guided practice, flexibility on your part is perhaps more important than at any other part of the lesson. During this time, it is very likely that things might not go as you planned. A willingness to roll with the punches is essential during guided practice. You may find yourself needing to back-pedal, to adjust course to address student misunderstandings that you may not have foreseen. In cases where you determine that the class is off track, you may have to interrupt small-group work to pull students back into direct instruction. Other times, you may need to provide more opportunities to practice during small group time. The important thing to understand here is that, in teaching, things don't always work out as planned. More often than not, this is revealed during guided practice. Flexibility, as opposed to a firm determination to execute your lesson plan to the letter, will benefit you (and your students) greatly in the long run.

Student's Role

In moving from direct instruction, where students are listening and absorbing information while the teacher presents, to guided practice, where students are more actively engaged in the work, it is important to consider the students' role in the lesson. Thinking about what students should be doing during guided practice can help you in your execution. These aren't necessarily things that will show up in your lesson plan. Rather they are norms and expectations that you should keep in mind for guided practice in every lesson that you teach.

Everyone Talks

During guided practice, all students should contribute to the discussion. This is true both for the whole-group and small-group portions. This ranges from all hands in the air when the entire class is asked a question to all students being involved in small-group discussions. Your goal during guided practice should be for all students to interact in the work, particularly in terms of speaking. The expectation is that all students will talk and engage.

Everyone Works

Discussion will not be the only aspect of guided practice. Writing, problem solving, and other forms of work will be involved. Whether it be taking notes, writing an answer to a question, or solving a problem, all students should also be engaged in the work.

A Note on Collaboration Norms

Working in groups is not something students should be expected to know how to do naturally. Structures and systems, including discussion protocols and expectations, need to be explained, modeled, and practiced. Depending upon the age of your students, this may involve an investment of time that carries over the course of several weeks.

But . . . it will be worth it. As Bambrick-Santoyo and colleagues write, "A conversation is like a soccer game: it's hard to move the ball up the field if your team doesn't know how to pass the ball" (2013, 55). Time spent working on the habits of discussion, engraining the routines that make up effective collaboration, will pay off in the form of more focused and impactful small-group work.

FAQ

How long should guided practice last?

Just as with direct instruction, there is no rule for the duration of guided practice. You want to provide enough time for students to participate in whole and small group work, as well as time for checking for understanding. Depending on the lesson, this may take as little as 10 or as much as 20 minutes. When planning, keep in mind that you want to allot enough time for students to engage in all the essential parts of guided practice, but in a way that also leaves enough time for them to practice the work independently, which may often require 20–30 minutes.

I'm having trouble keeping my students on task when they work in small groups. What can I do?

It's all about routines. Have you taught students how to work in small groups? Have you practiced the routines of guided practice such that students have mastered them? If students are off task, they may not understand what they're supposed to do. Even if you have practiced the routines, at times you'll need to pump the brakes and reinforce. This means more practice and more modeling. If the expectations are clearly stated, and the students have practiced and internalized the routines, your guided practice will flow a lot more smoothly, with fewer disruptions and with less confusion.

At the end of guided practice, my students are not demonstrating readiness for independent practice. What am I doing wrong?

Although it is good that you are thinking about your responsibility (rather than the students') in terms of a successful guided practice, don't be so hard on yourself! It might not be something you're doing "wrong" so much as something you need to tweak or tighten. One important question to consider is whether or not the work students are doing in guided practice is aligned to the objective and to the work you did during direct instruction. Lack of alignment can often lead to students getting off track. Another pitfall involves small group discussion. Are you making sure to save time for students to work in groups to answer a question or solve a problem? If so, are you providing enough time? Finally, reflect back upon the lessons that haven't gone well in this regard—did you ask questions that push students' thinking and that help you uncover their misconceptions? Asking questions that do these things is very important, and it can help you diagnose not only the misunderstandings of your students, but the parts of your lesson that need strengthening, as well.

Activity—Planning Guided Practice

Building upon your direct instruction plan from the activity in Chapter 5, use the following template to plan the guided practice.

Guided Practice:

Whole group:

Small group:

Scripted questions:

Checks for understanding:

7

Independent Practice

Independence is happiness.

—*Susan B. Anthony*

With two-thirds of your lesson planned, it is time to turn your attention to the final piece of the puzzle: independent practice. It is at this point of the lesson when the goal you've been working toward becomes a reality. The stage is now set. You have primed the pump for the final reveal. It is now time to complete the gradual release of responsibility onto the students. It is time for independent practice, the part of the lesson where students engage with the material on their own.

However, like the other parts of your lesson, a great deal of thought must go into the planning of independent practice. It is not enough to simply place the work in front of students and let them spend the next 30 minutes silently engaged. First of all, the work you assign during independent practice must be thoughtfully designed and represent the logical next step in the progression toward full student responsibility. Independent practice should be meaningful, not simple busy work. It should provide an opportunity for students to dig into the work in a way that goes beyond "filling time."

Independent practice also represents an opportunity to dig into the work side-by-side with targeted students, students whom you know will need support to complete the work. Finally, it represents an opportunity to plan for students who will need an extra push, students for whom 30 minutes worth of work will probably take 10.

All of these things must be taken into account in advance, as you plan the lesson. The more care you take in preparation of this section, the better your results will be on the end-of-lesson assessment you created in the beginning stages of your work. In this chapter, you will walk through this step by step, developing an understanding of independent practice, its essential elements, and the types of variations you will need to maximize student understanding.

Independent Practice: An Overview

While independent practice represents the culmination of your attempts to gradually release responsibility to the students, it is not an area of planning that should be taken lightly. In order to truly achieve your end results, your plans must go beyond "Students will complete numbers 1–45 on page 143." Your students will not benefit from vagueness anywhere in your lesson plan, but this is especially true of independent practice.

But it can be easy to think of independent practice as the teacher's time to sit back, maybe work the room a little, and let the students do their thing. Think about it this way—independent practice is your last opportunity of the lesson to support struggling students, a golden opportunity to support and challenge your "high flyers," and your chance to give your students the gift of time. Time, that precious and finite commodity, often leads us to rush through or cut short the opportunity to practice. Independent practice is the time when a great deal of differentiation takes place, something that requires a great deal of preparation and planning.

While the goal of independent practice is fairly straightforward—provide students with the opportunity to practice the work on their own—there are countless things to take into account in the planning stages. Key questions such as "What about students who get done early?" or "What about students who can't handle it on their own yet?" must be answered as you plan. Other considerations, such as alignment to the objective and the end-of-lesson assessment, are critical.

One key to successful independent practice is discussed by Doug Lemov (2010) in *Teach Like a Champion* . . . multiple at-bats. (An *at-bat* refers to an attempt or an instance of practice, so "multiple at-bats" essentially means opportunities to practice multiple times.) Lemov likens student work to that of a surgeon: "Want to know what single factor best predicts the quality of surgeon you select?" he asks. "It's not her reputation, not the place where she went to medical school, not even how smart she is. The best predictor is how many surgeries of the type you're having done that she's done. It's muscle memory. It's repetition" (2010, 104). In other words, if you want to give your students the opportunity to master a concept or skill, it's key that you provide them with time to practice it. Over and over.

A slightly more extreme take on this idea is provided by Malcolm Gladwell in his book *Outliers* (2011). In it, Gladwell states that the "10,000 Hour Rule" predicates success in a given area. In essence, this means that to achieve greatness, something needs to be practiced for 10,000 hours. He cites several examples, among them Bill Gates, who had 10,000 hours to practice programming on his first computer, and the Beatles, who performed for 10,000 hours in Hamburg, Germany, to perfect their sound before returning to England and then taking over the world of music.

The key takeaway for independent practice is this: if you want students to master something, you have to let them practice it. Doing so immediately after you've shown them how to do it during direct instruction and worked together with them during guided practice makes perfect sense.

Like so many ideas in education, the idea of multiple at-bats or hours and hours of practice isn't always practical or even feasible. Not every subject or topic lends itself to practicing it over and over. For example, if you want students to write an argumentative essay, you wouldn't have them write 40 of them in an effort to deem them "proficient" at writing this type of piece. That's just crazy talk! Just as with other instructional decisions, a balance is required—and there is certainly no one right way to make it happen.

What's most important is that the time for students to practice on their own is held sacred. It can be very tempting to want to devote large chunks of time during your lesson to modeling and practicing for and with students. This essentially prolongs the direct instruction and guided practice, though, and robs students of the opportunity to show you what they know. Strong pacing is a priority and we will discuss this and other challenges and pitfalls in the following sections of this chapter.

Teacher and Student Roles During Independent Practice

Just as with the other parts of your lesson plan, when planning for independent practice, it is important to think about what both the teacher and the students will be doing. In both instances, it is also critical to consider your end goal: mastery of the objective. Independent practice is the final step, the students' last opportunity to engage in the work before you assess their understanding.

The Teacher's Role

Monitoring and providing feedback become the teacher's primary tasks during independent practice. Neither of these will necessarily be written into a lesson plan, but they are important habits of instruction that deserve mention when thinking about this section of the lesson. What can be written into a lesson plan, though, are the interventions that you plan to have with students that might struggle. This should include preparing for possible misconceptions that students might have as well as preparing questions that will help them work through these misconceptions. (See the "Essentials of Independent Practice" for more on this.)

Monitoring

In terms of monitoring, your work here involves "working the room," moving from student to student to closely observe their work. During this time, you should also be asking probing questions to help push them to deeper understanding. It is critical that you intervene at the first sign of a student's struggles. The longer a student is stuck or confused, the more challenging it can be for him or her to "right the ship." You will know, of course, which students are most likely to struggle. Keeping a close eye on them as they complete their independent work is critical. But you should not assume that they are the only ones who will find the work difficult. Any student, at any time, can run into trouble with the work. Therefore, monitoring the entire class closely and intervening quickly whenever it is needed are important responsibilities of the teacher during independent practice.

Feedback

Providing feedback shifts you from a questioner to an asserter of opinions. But what is feedback, anyway? Let's start with what it isn't. General statements about a student's effort (e.g., "good job!") don't qualify as feedback. In fact, feedback should not be evaluative at all. Nor should it consist of giving tips or advice.

Two of the key elements of effective feedback, writes author and educator Grant Wiggins (2012), are that it's actionable and user-friendly. Actionable feedback is delivered in a way that lets students turn around and use it immediately. It can be feedback about something they should keep doing or something they should think about starting to do. Feedback is user-friendly when it makes sense to the student, and when it's delivered in the context of the work they are engaged in. Furthermore, to be user-friendly it needs to be limited in scope. Too much feedback can be overwhelming and confusing, and thus counterproductive.

Convening Small Groups

A final element of the teacher's role during independent practice involves convening small groups. This is done when needed, not necessarily every lesson. Bringing together a small group of students should be done when you observe students struggling. Sometimes all students will need is a gentle nudge in the proper direction so that they shift their thinking and change their approach.

The Student's Role

There is slightly more to the students' role than putting their noses to the grindstone and getting to work. Yes, they will be working on their own, working toward mastery of your objective. However, there are some norms around expectations that they should be aware of when it comes to independent practice.

The first expectation of students is that they have to be sure to ask questions. If there are aspects of the independent work that they find confusing or parts where they're stuck, they should know that now is the time to ask because their teacher will be willing and able to work side-by-side with them, if necessary. This behavior certainly is a reflection of your classroom culture. It is critical that you not only have built into your classroom norms that questions are OK, but also that students recognize that perseverance during independent work time is the expectation.

The other expectation for students, and one that also ties into classroom culture, can be demonstrated by author Lucy Calkins's (2007) mantra when working with students: "When you're done, you've just begun." What this translates to is that students should understand what to do when they've finished their independent work. Your well-planned direct instruction and guided practice will certainly lead to this outcome, so students have to know what to work on when they finish—and you have to have work for them to do as well. This best takes the form of challenge problems that are tied to the objective, allowing them to further deepen their understanding of the topic.

Essentials of Independent Practice

The prior two sections have given you an overview of what independent practice time should look like. Let's turn our attention back to planning and discuss the key considerations you should take into account when planning for this section of the lesson. In the rest of the chapter, I synthesize all that has been discussed thus far in the chapter as a means of helping you focus on effective planning.

Alignment

Just as in the other two sections, alignment to the objective is key. The work that students complete during independent practice should match the type of work they did during direct instruction and guided practice. This is true of both type and level of rigor. Unfamiliar work, or new types of problems or questions, should not show up for the first time in students' independent work. Challenge or extension problems certainly have their place. But that place is reached only after students have had an opportunity to practice the objective-aligned work on their own.

Intervention

Intervention can take place on an individual basis or in small groups, as described in "The Teacher's Role" section. You should write plans for intervention into your lesson plan as best you can. It's true that many of the decisions you make about intervention will be in-the-moment and based upon your observations of students and their work. However, you should make notes in your plans about the types of work you may want to use to engage struggling students. It might involve key parts of your lesson that you know you may want to revisit, or some skill-work that will help support students who might struggle with the new concept.

Enrichment

Take the opportunity in independent practice to do something that teachers often struggle to find the time to do—meet the needs of students who need more of a challenge. By writing into your lesson plan a strategy for addressing these students' needs, you will be prepared to differentiate their work. Coming up with enrichment work on the fly is never an easy thing to do. Take the time to plan and prepare so that the students that are ready for an extra challenge are provided with one.

Planning for Misunderstandings

This ties in with intervention. As mentioned in chapters 5 and 6, addressing student misunderstandings in your plan is very important. When planning independent practice (and direct instruction, and guided practice), ask yourself, "Where might my students have trouble? What mistakes might they make?" Devoting a short time to these questions in advance of your lesson will pay huge dividends. Anticipating these possible misunderstandings in advance will allow you to be on the lookout for them as you monitor and work with small groups.

Independence: Keeping Independent Practice Independent

Finally, it can be very challenging to resist the urge to let students work in collaborative groups during independent practice. However if they work in groups, when you assess their understanding at the end of the lesson, how will you be able to have confidence that the students can master the objective on their own? Collaborative work can and should be done during guided practice. In some cases, you will want this to be a large chunk of the lesson. The benefits of collaborative learning are well documented and I am certainly not recommending that this strategy should never be employed. However, in an effort to truly gauge which students understand and which do not, independent work is a necessity.

FAQ

How much time should be spent on independent practice?

You want the bulk of your lesson to be spent engaging students in the work. Aim for 20–30 minutes of independent practice each day. This will give you enough time to work with small groups, when needed, and give students enough time to practice so that they can demonstrate mastery on the end-of-lesson assessment.

What if the class consistently finishes their independent practice 10–15 minutes before the end of the period?

If students are finishing early on a regular basis, it's definitely a reason to examine your plans. There could be multiple causes. The one key question that will help you diagnose this issue: how are they doing on their exit tickets? If they are consistently mastering them as a group, it is possible that your lessons should be more rigorous and challenging. If the results are mediocre or mixed, you may need to provide more at-bats during independent practice. This could also mean that there are weaknesses in the design of the other parts of your lesson. Perhaps your lesson isn't aligned to the objective throughout. Perhaps the release of responsibility is happening suddenly, rather than gradually. Maybe your modeling and thinking aloud during direct instruction needs to be more explicit. When things don't go as planned . . . it's time to look at your plans.

What about projects? I have my students work on a lot of projects throughout the year and I'm not sure how this, or the other chapters of this book for that matter, applies.

Projects are a tremendous way to assess students' understanding. They can be incredibly engaging and exciting for students, too. Can projects fit within an *I do, we do, you do* format? I believe that they can. If your students are engaged in a project, each day you could model for them a new component of the project (direct instruction), have them practice this component together (guided practice), and then have them engage in this component on their own (independent practice). *Voila!* It won't fit perfectly every time, of course. When it comes to teaching, nothing fits perfectly every time. But if you are teaching something new, the gradual release planning approach can be very effective.

Activity: Planning for Independent Practice

Continuing your work from the previous chapters, complete your lesson plan by planning for independent practice.

Independent Practice:	
Potential misunderstandings:	
Interventions:	**Enrichment:**

Part IV
After the Lesson

Assessing Student Understanding

All assessment is a continual work in progress.

—*Linda Suskie*

Congratulations! Your lesson is complete. But, not surprisingly, there is work yet to be done. After the lesson, you will have amassed a stack of end-of-lesson assessments. It is now time to examine this data and use it to your students' advantage.

Recall, these end-of-lesson assessments were designed in such a way that they will go beyond simply who "got it" and who did not (see Chapter 4 for details). The assessments will reveal details about *why* misconceptions occurred. With this information in hand, you can now create a plan to address these misconceptions in the coming days or weeks.

Within this chapter, we will dive into a portion of the instructional process that just might have more of an impact upon student achievement than any other. The steps you take after the lesson is complete are key to uncovering students' thinking so that you can replace their misconception with understanding.

Looking at Student Work

You'll begin by examining students' exit assessments with the goal of determining who understood, who didn't, and why those students who didn't made mistakes. In this section, I'll share a general protocol for this process.

You should, of course, develop your own protocol for looking at student work based upon your own preferences and the needs of your students.

The First Sort

Sort the work into two piles, one for students who demonstrated full mastery (set these aside) and the other for those who did not. Because your lesson was so well designed (I am certain of this), you should have a large majority of students who showed that they completely understood.

The Second Sort

Examine the errors students made. Attempt to determine why students made the mistakes that they did. Sort the assessments into piles based upon common mistakes. For example, for a fifth-grade multiplication assessment, you might sort work into three categories: "Added instead of multiplied," "Forgot to regroup," or "Made a place value error."

Your categories from your second sort will in some, but not all, cases work into a neat grouping of a handful of misunderstandings. But this won't always be the case. Sometimes, it will be nearly impossible to determine why a student made a mistake. This can happen even when a very thoughtfully created exit ticket is used. These students most likely will need a one-on-one conference with you so that you can ask them questions that allow you to understand their thinking more clearly. They may need another chance at solving the problems, too.

In other cases, you'll determine that some students made multiple mistakes. For example, in the aforementioned multiplication exit tickets, you may have a student that *both* forgot to regroup and made a place value error. That student also may need a one-on-one conference, unless there are multiple students making the same mistakes. If so, these students can become a category of their own.

If your assessment includes any sort of writing, this can be an invaluable source of information during the second sort. Examine students' writing carefully. It can provide a great deal of insight into students' thinking about the work. If trends are revealed through the writing, this can help you refine your student groups so that the intervention is more focused and effective.

When the Majority of the Class Does not Show Mastery . . .

Regardless of how well planned or well executed your lesson was, there will come times when a large portion of your class will not be able to demonstrate mastery on your end-of-lesson assessment.

In this case, you may have to reteach the entire lesson (or the portion of the lesson that the data reveals was a challenge). However, the reteach should not be an exact replica of the original lesson. If it didn't work the first time, it probably won't the second time, right?

You will want to plan to use instructional strategies that are different from the original. This may or may not require you to completely rewrite the lesson. Depending upon your new strategies, you may be able to reuse your direct instruction, your guided practice, or both.

The challenge of keeping pace with your school or district's scope and sequence is always at the front of teachers' minds, so it merits discussion. It's my opinion that student understanding of grade-level standards is of primary importance. This is absolutely true when comparing to "staying on pace" or "not falling behind," two concerns that can cause a great deal of stress on teachers. It seems to me that stopping for a day to reteach when no one in the class understood is an excellent and strategic use of time. There are always ways of catching up, even if it's not in the short term. Student achievement should always trump any concerns of keeping up with a curriculum or pacing guide.

The Plan

At this point, you will create an intervention plan for each of these groups to specifically pinpoint and address their misunderstandings. This will involve both the when and the what of intervention. As with the reteach of the entire lesson, each intervention plan should involve an approach that differs from the original lesson.

In many cases, your plans for intervention will be straightforward. Most of the time, you'll be working with groups for less than 10 minutes. Your plans should not involve instruction that takes much longer than that. You might think that you'll need a full class period for each group, but that is probably not the case. Your intervention should be swift and focused, so that it allows students to take their new understanding and apply it to the current or next day's new work. In addition, it should happen as soon as possible following the end-of-lesson assessment. This means you'll want to intervene during the next school day's lesson, at the latest.

Depending upon what your examination reveals, there may also be cases where you're going to want to check in with students beyond the next school day. This may be based upon what you gleaned from the exit tickets or on prior performance in earlier lessons. Be sure to note these students so that you are sure to check in with them at later dates.

For each intervention group you plan, you should also prepare an assessment. Think of it as an end-of-group assessment or an exit ticket for the group work. This should be a quick assessment that takes very little time to complete. It should also be an assessment that will continue to reveal students' misunderstandings, if necessary, as these will need to be addressed as soon as possible.

Looking at Student Work Protocol

1. *First Sort*—Sort into two piles for those who mastered and those who did not.
2. *Second Sort*—Sort into categories based upon students' errors.
3. *The Plan*—Create an intervention plan for these groups that targets students' misunderstandings.

Structures for Intervention

Finding the time to execute intervention can be a challenge, but it is well worth it. Without it, students might fall further and further behind and be unable to meet the standards for your unit of study or even for your school year. A skillfully crafted intervention plan keeps all students on track, preventing these falling-behind scenarios from occurring.

One way of making this work is to pull these intervention groups during the next day's direct instruction. During this time you can, very briefly, execute your plan and reassessment. In addition, if these are students you think might have trouble with the current day's content, you can check for understanding while you have them with you and intervene around the day's work if necessary. This will allow you to support them early on during the independent practice, hopefully correcting course and steering them toward mastery on the end-of-lesson assessment.

The Case for Intervention Blocks

In many schools, a block of time is set aside for specifically addressing students' individual needs. These needs are determined by the end-of-lesson (and end-of-week or end-of-unit) assessments. By carving out time in your classroom or school's schedule for specific time for intervention, you will impact student achievement in a meaningful way.

Response to Intervention (RTI) is a popular program that is implemented in many schools. RTI calls these intervention times "Tier 2" interventions. They take place after the original teaching (Tier 1) has taken place. As Jim Wright writes in *The RTI Toolkit*, "the primary focus of Tier 2 interventions is the classroom" (2007, iv). In other words, your intervention should ideally take place during the regular lesson. However, sometimes even these Tier 2 interventions don't work. That's when the Tier 3 intervention block, an intervention strategy that occurs separate from and outside of the classroom, comes in.

If you use centers or stations in your classroom, another means of providing support to students is by differentiating work that they complete during this time. Setting up a center or station where students pull work from their own folder—work that the teacher selects based upon what each student needs to practice—is a way to provide extra practice on work concepts they may have previously struggled with.

In a case where you have a majority of students struggling on the exit ticket, that assessment can become a great warm-up, starter, or Do Now for the next day's lesson. Five minutes spent re-trying, re-explaining, and discussing the work again before the following day's instruction may be all that's needed to address and remove most, if not all, misunderstandings. At the very least, this process can lead to a majority of students demonstrating mastery, allowing you to form intervention groups from the students who haven't done so yet.

Extension Options

There will be students who do not require intervention and it is important to keep them in mind when planning after a lesson. That way, it won't only be your struggling students who are getting the support they need. Students who clearly demonstrate understanding should be differentiated for, as well.

In cases such as these, providing students with extension and enrichment questions or a challenging performance task can work to deepen their thinking and understanding. If possible, find time during independent practice, while you are working with intervention groups, to meet with these students as well. This time can be used to check in on the day's work and also provide and explain the enrichment work. That way, you are meeting all students where they are, supporting their individual needs and driving achievement at the same time.

The Role of Homework

Cases for and against homework can be made. In fact, homework has become a bit of a divisive topic in education circles. In *The Case Against Homework*, Bennett and Kalish (2007) argue that homework has become a task filled with drudgery, causing parents consternation and stealing important time for exercise and play from children. They cite a 2004 University of Michigan study that showed that the amount of time students spend doing homework has increased 51 percent since 1981 (p. 11).

Furthermore, research studies on homework have yielded inconsistent results, not revealing that homework is *never* effective, but rather that *in many cases* it is not effective (Vatterot 2009). Vatterot suggests that teachers "should reflect carefully on [homework's] purpose, plan the nature of the task carefully, and assess homework carefully to check for understanding. . . . Children are not seeds in a petri dish or rats in a maze. They are dynamic, thinking, feeling human beings, each with unique learning needs" and thus an effective and thoughtful homework plan is a necessity (2009, 86).

Many teachers will also tell you that the process of assigning, collecting, and grading homework can be frustrating. At times, it can be a struggle to get all students to complete the work and turn it in. Running copies and checking all those papers can be time consuming as well—time that would be better spent on planning. This is especially true if you have to factor in low rates of return.

That being said, homework can serve as an effective means of providing students who need support with extra practice. The three keys to getting the most out of homework assignments are *individualization, brevity,* and *independence.* Work sent home can be individualized to meet the needs of your different learning groups. This work should also not take an inordinate amount of time. Finally, it should be work of the type that students have worked on in school and can complete independently. Homework must be thought of as an opportunity for extra practice, rather than an assignment of busy work. By making sure you meet the criteria for effective homework, you will avoid this pitfall and your homework will benefit students, rather than overwhelm them.

Elements of Effective Homework

1. Individualized
2. Brief
3. Independent

FAQ

You recommend pulling groups during classroom instruction, but there just isn't time . . . how do I do it?

Think of it this way: if you plan your lesson for a 5–7 minute direct-instruction period, 10–15 minutes of guided practice, and 30–45 minutes of independent practice, you can easily work with groups during independent practice for 5–7 minutes each. True, you may not be able to work with every student every day, but if you plan your time accordingly, you will be able to see every student multiple times per week.

My school has a homework plan firmly in place. It conflicts with your suggestions and my own personal philosophy. What should I do?

The first step would be to raise your concerns with the decision maker(s) that put the plan into place. Ask them about their rationale and explain your own thinking. If the rationale is that parents want it, is there data or evidence to support this? If the rationale is that students need the extra practice or that they should all be doing the same assignments, share the idea about individualization based upon assessment data as a means of intervention and/or enrichment. If you truly do not have the freedom to assign the type of homework you want in a manner that is best for students, this is definitely a conversation worth having.

Can the Looking at Student Work protocol be executed among a group of teachers?

Absolutely! It especially works wonders when teachers have all given a common end-of-lesson assessment. Student work can be sorted not only by class, but also by grade to identify trends that exist in all classrooms. If the logistics work, this can lead to students being grouped across classrooms as they are at Mesquite Elementary in Tucson, Arizona. At Mesquite, after an end-of-week assessment, students rotate to different classrooms for reteaching or enrichment, based upon their performance on the assessment (Noburi 2011; Mesquite Elementary School 2011).

A collaborative approach to Looking at Student Work can also open up conversations about teaching strategies. The participating team can discuss how they taught particular concepts, sharing ideas about what worked and what didn't.

Activity: Planning from Student Work

Using a set of end-of-lesson assessments, follow the three-step protocol described earlier in the chapter. Then complete the following action plan to address your students' misunderstandings. The template should be modified based upon the number of groups you have.

Group 1 Students	Group 2 Students	Group 3 Students
Focus of instruction (based upon misconceptions)		
Timeline (when intervention will occur)		
Instructional strategies		

Conclusion

Success occurs when opportunity meets preparation.

—*Zig Ziglar*

I opened this book with the confession that lesson planning wasn't always my top priority when I was a classroom teacher. I have come to realize, however, that a well-designed and well-executed lesson that engages every learner and leads to student mastery and understanding is not something that comes out of thin air. Behind every great lesson is a great lesson plan. Without a plan (or with one that is haphazardly written), you are simply rolling the dice, hoping that students will learn. Student achievement is not something we should be gambling on. Instead, we should be doing everything in our power as educators to ensure achievement happens with all of our students. This starts with a plan.

The demands that are placed upon today's educators are numerous, to say the least. For teachers, time can seem like a resource of which there is never enough. Finding time to craft strong lesson plans is, without a doubt, an enormous challenge. But it is time well spent, and so an examination of your weekly schedule may be in order so that you can prioritize this very important practice.

This does not mean, however, that lesson planning needs to be the next step on your road to burnout. Making sure to find the balance that works best for you is of the utmost importance. Planning should never require so much of your energy that it takes away from your ability—including your patience, flexibility, and determination—to deliver an effective lesson.

One key thing to remember is that your plans should not only suit your students' needs, but yours as well. Some teachers will need to script out several key parts of their lesson, planning exactly what they want to say and when they want to say it. Others are able to boil down the lesson into its key parts and write a much shorter plan. Still others opt for a combination of each. Whichever iteration works for you, the goal remains the same: student mastery of the objective.

Hopefully the chapters of this book have strengthened your knowledge of a set of lesson-planning essentials. This is not to say that this is the only or best way to plan instruction. A lesson plan should always be designed in a way that will lead to student mastery. The method I've presented might not—no, *should not*—work for every situation. Think of this book as a starting point, a guide from which to begin strengthening your lesson plans. Over time, your approach may evolve and your planning template may look very different than the one I've shared in this book (see Appendix A for a full template). What matters most is that you are planning for all of your students' success in advance of the lesson.

Appendix A
Lesson Plan Template

This template attempts to put all the different chapters of the book together into one document. While this might not suit the specific needs of every teacher or every lesson, it can serve as a starting point upon which to build a template that works best for you, your lesson, and your students.

Date: Teacher: Class/Subject:	Standard:
Objective:	
End-of-Lesson Assessment:	
Potential Student Misunderstandings:	
Direct Instruction: *Modeling:* *Think-Alouds:* *Check for Understanding:*	
Guided Practice: *Whole-Group:* *Small-Group:* *Scripted Questions:* *Checks for Understanding:*	
Independent Practice:	
Interventions:	**Enrichment:**
Notes:	

Appendix A
Lesson Plan Template

Appendix B
A Note to School Leaders

Together we can do great things.

—*Mother Teresa*

Much of this book is written with classroom teachers in mind. However, there is much that school leaders, including principals and instructional coaches, can glean from this approach to planning. Individual teachers will hopefully be inspired to improve their planning after reading this book. But school leaders have the ability to impact multiple teachers (and, in turn, multiple groups of students) by developing strong school-wide lesson planning expectations. A well-communicated vision and standard of excellence for lesson planning that disseminates from a school's leaders will have a profound impact on teaching and learning.

Prioritizing strong lesson planning (and effective use of end-of-lesson assessments) indicates a dedication to student achievement. Setting aside time to not only review teachers' lesson plans, but also to observe their execution, can be challenging—school leaders are constantly pulled in multiple directions. But it is sure to be time well spent as it will impact every student in the school.

Five ideals make up my recommended approach for school leaders when it comes to lesson planning: emphasizing the purpose, scheduling the time, conducting observation and feedback, creating time and structure for teachers, and providing professional development.

Emphasizing the Purpose

A great deal of thought must go into all the parts of a school-wide emphasis on strong lesson planning. It is possible, though, that none is more important than communicating the purpose of this emphasis. It is critical that teachers understand the *why* of lesson planning. They need to know that it's worth their time and that it will actually make a difference. Otherwise, a lesson plan becomes an activity of compliance. Without an understanding of purpose, the plan is simply yet another form for teachers to complete. In the eight chapters of this book, I attempted to expose and explain the intricacies of a strong lesson plan.

I also tried to communicate the purpose of each aspect of planning. This will be critical for you to do, as well, in order to support teachers in writing high-quality plans.

Scheduling the Time

If you're a school leader, you don't need me telling you that there is never enough time in a day to accomplish everything. This is something you know firsthand. It may not seem like it, however, but you have control over your schedule and the things that you prioritize for your school.

Making time to review lesson plans and conduct observations (described in the following section) is an absolute necessity for school leaders.

Conducting Observations

It's one thing to look at a plan for instruction on paper. Seeing that lesson plan in execution can be a game-changer for a school leader. Observing teachers bringing plans to life can be exhilarating and can provide insight into their planning process. It can also aid you in identifying trends, both in teacher practice and student behavior.

Your observations needn't be long. In *Rethinking Teacher Supervision and Evaluation*, Kim Marshall (2013) recommends 5–15 minute "mini-observations" so that you are able to observe every classroom teacher at least 10 times per year. Marshall also suggests that all observations should be accompanied by feedback as soon as possible. This can consist of a short meeting accompanied by written or emailed notes. These feedback meetings should also be built into your weekly schedule, so that both the observation and the opportunity for conversation are prioritized.

The feedback meeting also serves as an opportunity to provide face-to-face feedback on lesson plans, both those for the week and the one that was taught during the mini-observation. This time to talk with the teacher enables you to ask about the parts of the lesson you didn't observe, including the results of the end-of-lesson assessment and the plan for students who did not demonstrate mastery. Even further, it could involve tackling a planning concern or challenge side-by-side with teachers during this time. Combined with reviewing lesson plans, this cycle of observation and feedback can have immediate and lasting impact upon both teacher practice and student performance.

A Note on Culture

A culture of observation and feedback is something that needs cultivating. Many teachers are not used to such frequent visits from school leaders. This can become intimidating, especially if teachers fear that these observations are evaluative and that they might impact their performance review or, even worse, their employment.

As a school leader, you must emphasize (sometimes repeatedly) that your observation and feedback cycle is informal, non-evaluative, and intended to support their development. If you desire a school culture where everyone is consistently striving to improve, you have to be the standard bearer, clearly communicating the purpose and living it yourself by sharing your own willingness to get better at your work.

Creating Time and Structures

Lesson planning takes time. As a school leader, this is something you have to recognize and value—and teachers should know you value it. This can be accomplished by setting up structures so that teachers have the opportunity to work on their plans. This can be done during grade-level meetings or during professional development days. It can also be done by taking things off teachers' plates that other personnel, including yourself, can do instead, such as lunch or recess duty. Every teacher knows that his or her job is not a traditional 9-to-5. That doesn't mean they should work 60 or more hours a week; this will only lead to frustration and burnout. You have the ability to carve out time during teachers' workdays so that they have time to plan and prepare. By making it happen, your teachers will be better able to write effective lesson plans for their students.

Providing Professional Development

As an instructional leader, it is also important for you to recognize the value of developing your staff. When it comes to lesson planning, this starts with the understanding that simply telling teachers to fill out a lesson plan template is not enough. You must go beyond telling to teaching, providing teachers with the support and understanding necessary to write strong plans.

This can be accomplished by setting aside time for collaborative practice during staff meetings or development days. This might involve a year-long deep dive into the individual portions of a lesson, perhaps exploring one a month during staff meetings. It can also be supported by providing exemplar plans so that teachers have a clear benchmark in mind when writing their own plans.

References

Ainsworth, Larry. 2004. *Unwrapping the Standards: A Simple Process to Make Standards Manageable*. Lanham, MD: Advanced Learning Press.

Alberti, Sandra. 2012/2013. "Making the Shifts." *Educational Leadership* 70 (4, December/January): 24–27. http://www.ascd.org/publications/educational-leadership/dec12/vol70/num04/Making-the-Shifts.aspx.

Bambrick-Santoyo, Paul, Aja Settles, and Juliana Worrell. 2013. *Great Habits, Great Readers: A Practical Guide for K-4 Reading in the Light of Common Core*. New York: Jossey-Bass.

Bennett, Sara and Nancy Kalish. 2007. *The Case Against Homework: How Homework Is Hurting Children and What Parents Can Do About It*. New York: Harmony Books.

Black, P.J., C. Harrison, C. Lee, B. Marshall, and D. Wiliam. (2002) *Working Inside the Black Box: Assessment for Learning in the Classroom*. London, UK: King's College, London School of Education.

Black, P.J., and D. Wiliam. (1998). "Inside the Black Box: Raising Standards through Classroom Assessment." *Phi Delta Kappa* (October): 1–13. Retrieved from http://csi.idso.eportalnow.net/uploads/1/1/3/2/11323738/inside_the_black_box_1998.pdf.

Blackburn, Barbara R. 2012. *Rigor Is NOT a Four-Letter Word*, 2nd ed. New York: Routledge Eye on Education.

Calkins, Lucy. 2007. *Units of Study for Teaching Writing, Grades 3–5*. Portsmouth, NH: Heinemann.

Chappuis, Stephen, and Jan Chappuis. 2008. "The Best Value in Formative Assessment." *Educational Leadership*, 65 (4): 14–19.

Fisher, Douglass and Nancy Frey. 2008. *Better Learning Through Structured Teaching*. Alexandria, VA: ASCD.

Fisher, Douglass and Nancy Frey. 2011. *The Purposeful Classroom*. Alexandria, VA: ASCD.

Gladwell, Malcolm. 2011. *Outliers: The Story of Success*. New York: Back Bay Books.

Hattie, John. 2012. *Visible Learning for Teachers: Maximizing Impact on Learning*. New York: Routledge.

Hu, Winnie. 2011. "State Takeovers of Other Districts Have Had Mixed Results." *The New York Times*, December 11, http://www.nytimes.com/2011/12/12/education/state-takeovers-of-school-districts-have-had-mixed-results.html?_r=0.

Johnson, R.T., and D.W. Johnson. (1986). "Action Research: Cooperative Learning in the Science Classroom." *Science and Children*, 24: 31–32.

Lake, Robin J., Ashley Jocim, and Michael DeArmond. 2015. "Fixing Detroit's Broken School System." *Education Next*, 15 (1). Retrieved from http://educationnext.org/fixing-detroits-broken-school-system/.

Lemov, Doug. 2010. *Teach Like a Champion*. San Francisco: Jossey-Bass.

Lemov, Doug. 2014. "I Like Turn and Talk as Much as the Next Guy, But….," *Teach Like a Champion* (blog), March 25, http://teachlikeachampion.com/blog/like-turn-talk-much-next-guy/.

Liben, David, and Meredith Liben. 2014. "'Both and' Literacy Instruction," Achieve the Core, April 12, http://achievethecore.org/page/687/both-and-literacy-instruction.

Maloch, Beth, and Randy Bomer. 2013. "Informational Texts and the Common Core Standards: What Are We Talking about, Anyway?" *Language Arts*, 90 (3): 205–13.

Marshall, Kim. 2013. *Rethinking Teacher Supervision and Evaluation: How to Work Smart, Build Collaboration, and Close the Achievement Gap*, 2nd ed. New York: Jossey-Bass.

Marzano, Robert. 2011. "Art and Science of Teaching: Objectives That Students Understand." *Educational Leadership*, 68 (8): 86–87.

Mesquite Elementary School. 2011. "Reteach and Enrich: How to Make Time for Every Student" (video), *Edutopia*, October 6, http://www.edutopia.org/stw-differentiated-instruction-budget-assessment-video.

Mishra, R. P. 2009. *Lesson Planning*. New Delhi, India: APH Publishing.

Moss, Connie M. and Susan M. Brookhart. 2012. *Learning Targets: Helping Students Aim for Understanding in Today's Lesson*. Alexandria, VA: ASCD.

Moss, Connie M., Susan M. Brookhart, and Beverly Long. 2011. "Knowing Your Learning Target." *Educational Leadership*, 68 (6): 66–69.

National Governors Association Center for Best Practices, Council of Chief State School Officers. 2010. Common Core State Standards, http://www.corestandards.org, accessed March 15, 2015.

NCTE Assessment Task Force. (2013). *Formative Assessment That Truly Informs Instruction*. Urbana, IL: National Council of Teachers of English. Retrieved from http://www.ncte.org/library/NCTEFiles/Resources/Positions/formative-assessment_single.pdf.

Nobori, Moriko. 2011. "5 Strategies to Ensure Student Learning," *Edutopia*, August 29, http://www.edutopia.org/stw-differentiated-instruction-budget-assessment-how-to.

Partnership for Assessment of Readiness for College and Careers. 2015. PARCC Task Prototypes and New Sample Items for ELA/Literacy, http://www.parcconline.org/samples/ELA.

Pearson, P. David, and Margaret C. Gallagher. 1983, October. *Technical Report No. 297: The Instruction of Reading Comprehension*. Urbana-Champaign: University of Illinois Center for the Study of Reading. Accessed June 20, 2015, https://www.ideals.illinois.edu/bitstream/handle/2142/17939/ctrstreadtechrepv01983i00297_opt.pdf?sequence=1.

Smarter Balanced Assessment Consortium. n.d. Sample Items and Performance Tasks. Accessed June 20, 2015, http://www.smarterbalanced.org/sample-items-and-performance-tasks/.

Student Achievement Partners. n.d. Achieve the Core. Accessed June 21, 2015, http://www.achievethecore.org.

Student Achievement Partners. n.d. "Common Core State Standards Shifts in Mathematics" and "Common Core Shifts for English Language Arts/Literacy." *Achieve the Core*. http://achievethecore.org/content/upload/122113_Shifts.pdf.

Vatterott, Cathy. 2009. Rethinking Homework: Best Practices That Support Diverse Needs. Alexandria, VA: ASCD.

Vygotsky, L.S. 1978. *Mind in Society: The Development of Higher Psychological Processes*. Cambridge, MA: Harvard University Press.

Webb, N. 1985. "Student Interaction and Learning in Small Groups: A Research Summary." In *Learning to Cooperate, Cooperating to Learn*, edited by Rachel Hertz Lazarowitz, Spencer Kagan, Shlomo Sharan, Robert Slavin, Clark Webb, and Richard Schmuck, 148–72. New York: Plenum Press.

Wiggins, Grant. 1989. "Teaching to the (Authentic) Test." *Educational Leadership*. April: 41–47.

Wiggins, Grant. 2012. "Seven Keys to Effective Feedback." *Educational Leadership*, 70 (1): 10–16.

Wiggins, Grant, and Jay McTighe. 2005. *Understanding by Design*, 2nd ed. Alexandria, VA: ASCD.

Wood, D., J. S. Bruner, and G. Ross. 1976. "The Role of Tutoring and Problem Solving." *Journal of Child Psychology and Psychiatry*, 17: 89–100.

Wood, D., and D. Middleton. 1975. "A Study of Assisted Problem-Solving." *British Journal of Psychology*, 66 (2): 181–91.

Wright, Jim. 2007. *The RTI Toolkit: A Practical Guide for Schools*. Port Chester, NY: National Professional Resources.

Zemelman, Steven, Harvey "Smokey" Daniels, and Arthur Hyde. 2012. *Best Practice: Bringing Standards to Life in America's Classrooms*. Portsmouth, NH: Heinemann.